CW00553942

Ottakar's LOCAL HISTORY *Series*

Cirencester

Cirencester Church from S.E.

Ottakar's LOCAL HISTORY Series

Cirencester

Compiled by
Sue Emson and Michael Bull

OTTAKAR'S

St John's Hospital

Contributors: Mary Bartlett, Mary Baynham, Bill Charlton, Tony Clack, Michael B. Clarke, Hilda Crawford, E.W. Fletcher, Brian Gegg, David Grace, Peter Grace, P. Griffiths, Jan Gronow, Lorna Lane, Josephine Morales, Tim Page, Vicki Ponsford, Mary Pridgeon, Barbara Read, Peter Rowe, Ralph Smith, Jacqui Stearn, Jim Thompson, Pauline Trevallian, David Viner, Emmeline Walls, Macolm Whitaker.

First published 2002

Tempus Publishing Limited
The Mill, Brimscombe Port,
Stroud, Gloucestershire, GL5 2QG

British Library Cataloguing in Publication Data.
A catalogue record for this book is available from the British Library.

ISBN 0 7524 2662 1

Typesetting and origination by Tempus Publishing Limited
Printed in Great Britain by Midway Colour Print, Wiltshire

Contents

Acknowledgements   6

Introduction   7

1. Civil War   9

2. The Union Man   13

3. Memories of the Rajah   16

4. Oxen in the Park   24

5. School Days   36

6. Wartime Memories   46

7. Shops, Pubs and Hostelries   65

8. All Things Bright and Beautiful   79

9. Pool and Porters   103

10. Around Cirencester   121

Cirencester Market Place, 1877.

Acknowledgements

We are enormously indebted to everyone who submitted articles, provided photographs or simply came to talk to us – without them there would have been no book. We are very grateful to the Revd Stanley Emson, not only for his invaluable expertise, but also for the many hours spent helping us organize and present the material. Members of Ottakar's staff Cirencester, notably Peter Giffin, Euan Greig and Gemma Ludbrook, have been more than generous with their time, enthusiasm and support. We would also like to thank the *Wilts and Gloucestershire Standard* for allowing us to reproduce photographs.

Introduction

Every community has its own history and we make it all the time. It is no longer just the stuff of kings and bishops and armies (it never really was, of course) but is just as much the daily fare of you and me as we go about our daily lives. Take this rich ingredient and add the ever-increasing interest in tracing our family history and the result is a rich cornucopia of the national and the local, of the economic and the social, and of the workplace and the home.

We look over our shoulders in order to see what has gone before, and usually as a way of understanding what is happening now. That might be how a village celebrated a jubilee (now and in the past) or how part of the town once looked when the railway station was still open and before the by-pass was built. The public institutions which look after our records, official as well as personal, are witness to a growing demand for access to their holdings. Computerisation of such records and the digitisation of images of all kinds is a current, and welcome, activity, drawing in funds for the purpose from national sources, so that this demand can be met whilst at the same time the fragile, ephemeral and often priceless original material can be saved from all this handling and use. Record keeping is only useful if it always has an eye on the future as well as the present and the past.

Cirencester's long and rich history has had the attention of many writers – archaeologists and historians perhaps in equal measure – and one might think that the ground has been pretty much worked over. This is not true. It might seem odd to say that the town has been relatively little written about, but by comparison with many others of its size and historical importance, this is the case. Why is that? One reason is that there is often an assumption that the task is too big to tackle and so a start is never made. But like the walk around the world, historical research can and does start with a single step, the first enquiry, from which everything else follows, all of it taken a step at a time. The trick is to know (or find out) in which order to make the steps and where and when, and the rest will follow in its turn. Nor need this be a solitary activity. The best historians share their material (what's the point otherwise?) and there is nothing quite so rewarding as others contributing bits of information or leads to follow, which help our own work along the way.

So it is with local and community history. People start with what they know, or what they remember (or think they remember) and then ask questions about it. Who moved the town's High Cross into the local park and when? Where was it originally? Was the town's arts centre once part of a brewery? When was the railway station actually closed, and do you remember the stationmaster, always with his red rose buttonhole? Out of this enquiry and research comes more information, shaped into a coherent whole and presented as a talk to a local group perhaps, or a publication of some sort. These days publication is not the impossible dream it must once have seemed. Technology can make it simpler rather than harder to accumulate data and make it available in an intelligible and interesting form.

It would be a poor community which didn't have such detailed studies and investigation going on all the time. People get an enthusiasm for what they want to know and stay with it to a conclusion. So it was that in Cirencester, amongst many other examples, the special history of the town's theatre was written (1993) and its equally special Quaker community (1998). To celebrate the Millennium (which triggered a mass of marvellous local history writing all over the country) the inhabitants of one street in Cirencester produced their own history, a classic in how to plan such a thing, carry it out and – even better – get it done at just the right time. So the parts add up to the whole. Standard, all-embracing town histories may be harder and harder to write, in the way in which our Victorian predecessors loved to do, but the accumulated evidence of such varied community life is a good alternative achievement.

That's the context for this book; a mixture of memories, the setting down of personal experiences and the 'looking over the shoulder' response to those who have gone before. It is as much about the people who have written these contributions as about their subject matter, just as the promoters of the project intended. Ottakar's are to be congratulated for promoting the 'write your own history' idea and in selecting Cirencester for inclusion. The response has proved that decision to be a good one.

Here are the fruits of researches into the life of the town, on pubs, schools and churches not surprisingly, but also on clubs (for which the town has a great tradition) and social activities. Did you know, for example, that Cirencester has the oldest surviving open-air swimming pool in the country, opened as long ago as 1869? It is one of the facts I've held onto since childhood, to go with the memories of the bracing experience of diving into the pool at the behest of a harassed teacher.

Some of the town's special places have drawn forth research. For a generation which still remembers, the story of evacuees in Cirencester remains a memorable episode. Others may have been intrigued about the white Rajahs, mysterious folk who lived here (some of the time) but were also an important part of a little-known bit of pink on the map of empire. Another simple fact is that oxen survived in use as beasts of burden in Cirencester Park almost as long (if not as long) as anywhere else in England, and here are the reminiscences of that story, now nationally important as well as locally fascinating.

Memories are important; we all have them. This volume – like the others in this local history series from Tempus nationwide – shows that we can and should set them down as a record, of interest to ourselves now and to others in the future. It seems the least we can do for the experience of living in such an interesting and historically rich town, doesn't it?

The Local Studies Collections at the Bingham Library and the Corinium Museum, both in Cirencester, are good sources of material; so too the Gloucestershire Record Office in Gloucester, which houses the major archives of the county. The principal societies are the Cirencester Archaeological and Historical Society (founded in 1955) which undertakes research projects, the Cirencester Family History Society which is the forum for family historians, and the Living Memory Historical Association, which specialises in the Second World War period. All three welcome new members and details are available from the above archives on request. Meanwhile, enjoy your research, whatever it may be!

David Viner
Chairman, Cirencester Archaeological & Historical Society
August 2002

1 Civil War

A town besieged

With colours blazing, pikes and muskets at the ready, and great hollers of 'God and England! God and England!' resounding through the tiny, crooked streets of Cirencester, the English Civil War was being not so much re-enacted as re-lived.

Cirencester was commemorating the 350th anniversary of the storming of the town in 1643 during the bloody English Civil War, the culmination of which was the beheading of King Charles I. Flourishing orange and red sashes, gold braids, extravagantly feathered hats, wearing only authentic type clothing of the period, the members of the English Civil War and Sealed Knot Societies marched from Cecily Hill into Market Place, following the exact route taken by the invading Royalist army led by Prince Rupert 350 years before. In the political struggle between the Royalists and Parliamentarians, more commonly known as the Cavaliers and Roundheads, Cirencester had clearly declared itself for Parliament. In the 1600s, it was considered a key rural town controlling important roads and river crossings and had a population of about 3,500, many of whom were involved in the cloth trade. The King is quoted as saying that in the area 'great quantities of cloth, canvas and locherame are to be had for supplying the great necessities our soldiers have for suits.'

The problems between the King and Parliament were mainly religious and financial. There was growing conflict within the church

and the King was financially weak. Several methods of raising money for the King had proved to be unpopular with the people and had met with considerable opposition.

Despite the fact that the citizens of Cirencester were determined to fight for their cause, they were, of course, country folk living everyday country folk lives and had no experience in the 'schoole of war.' But the harsh realities of war were now upon them.

With the threat of invasion by the Royalist army imminent, Cirencester fortified itself with soldiers, volunteers and five cannons strategically placed about the town. The desperate community barricaded the entrances to the town as best it could with wagon loads of bushes and with chains across the roads to prevent horses entering. Unfortunately, many of the town's best musketeers and cannoneers had been drawn away in the defence of nearby Sudely Castle, leaving their defences sadly depleted.

It may be that the citizens were resolute in their decision to stand firm against the invaders because they had been misled by their town leaders into believing that the Royalists were no more than 'a rabble of poore ragged fellowes' However, the Royalist army which stood in the vicinity of Cirencester on the 31 January 1643, was something very different. 7,000 cavalry, soldiers and musketeers led by the King's nephew Prince Rupert, an experienced, daring and charismatic soldier, who, having complete disregard for personal danger was known as the 'Mad Cavalier'. He

Civil War.

Preparing for battle, 1993.

'could lead cavalry like a man possessed... and in the storming of fortified towns he had no equal.'

During the dawn hours of 1 February, the Royalist troops surrounded the town. A heavy snow had fallen. As the townspeople watched the fires from the enemy camps in the nearby fields, their fear and apprehension can only be guessed at. Cirencester lay almost for the taking. At noon on Thursday 2 February 1643, Prince Rupert launched his attack. The barricades were broken down and set on fire. The pikes marched forward and turning aside the wagon loads of bushes, advanced into the town crying 'The town is ours.' When the people saw 'such numbers of gallant Gentry come upon them, their hearts sunke within them...' The residents were encountered immediately, some now running, and fourteen were killed then. Marksmen and snipers shot at the advancing army from upper windows and from the church tower. The inhabitants fought fiercely, for the eye witness account of Prince Rupert's chaplain says 'we must have disputed every wall and garden with them...' Then the King's whole troop advanced driving the townsfolk before them, killing many, and entered the Market Place. A 'Gentleman then shot another, who in his reeling, cryed 'Dogges, Dogges, Dogges... till the mudde stopt up his mouth'. At this point, one of the town's cannoneers, a Spaniard, came running out of the King's Head to fire on the Prince's troop as it approached but, 'He was slain by a Gentleman that rode in betwixt the Spaniard and his cannon, and Pistol'd him.' The superior cannon power of the Royalists eased their impending victory, for Rupert's reinforcements had included two mortars which fired explosive shells - a secret weapon indeed – and the shot was fired at random in the town causing fearful noise and terror. There were brave and heroic acts that day. A simple clothier of the town named Hodgkinson Paine was killed, defiantly holding the flag aloft: 'Then was Payne (a clothier) killed, with a Colours in his hand.' But also cowardly acts, as one, self-styled Captain Buck left town under the pretence of fetching in reinforcements, but not before he endeavoured to string up Humphrey Jasper, the vicar of a nearby village from the sign-post of the King's Head in the Market Place. The vicar was fortunately saved but Captain Buck escaped.

Notwithstanding the courage and daring of the people of Cirencester, at about 4 o'clock in the afternoon, the town was defeated. About 300 citizens lay dead. The dead and wounded left where they fell and about 1,200 prisoners were taken. According to a Parliamentary eyewitness, the conquering army plundered and looted the town and the prisoners taken 'were all turned that night into the church, and though many of them were wounded and weary, yet their friends were not suffered to bring them a cup of water into the church that night, but what they thrust in at the back of the church, having broken the windowes'. The following day, the army tied all the prisoners with ropes and marched them on foot through the mud to Oxford 'which in regard of the many horses, were up to their knees sometimes.'

The battle for Cirencester may have been won but the war was not and raged on until 1651. The Parliamentarians under Oliver Cromwell, a relatively unknown Puritan farmer who also proved himself to be a military genius, eventually defeated the Royalists and King Charles I was beheaded in 1649 (his death warrant is extant in Westminster Palace).

On the chilly but thankfully peaceful evening of 2 February 1993, the exact anniversary of the day when, in 1643, 1,200 wretched prisoners including the vicar were locked into Cirencester church, today's townspeople crowded into their parish church in the Market Place to hear a commemorative lecture, 'The Taking of Cirencester.' The past seemed real and near as musicians played music of the seventeenth century and slides were shown of the flamboyant 'Mad Cavalier' Prince Rupert, the elegant King Charles and the robust Oliver Cromwell. The register of deaths for February 1643 was open to view and many members of the congregation recognized their family name amongst those who fell. But most poignant was a fresh, green wreath placed that morning under a wall plaque inscribed 'Here lyeth buried ye body of Hodgkinson Paine clothier, who died the 3rd February, 1643… by death to life, by warre to peace for ever.'

Sources:

Biblioteca Gloucestrensis Vol. 2. A compilation of Civil War Tracts by J. Wasbourne, 1825.

A Relation of the Taking of Cirencester. London 1643. Parliamentary version. Account by John White.

A Particular Relation of the Action before Cirencester 1642 (1643). Royalist version.

Note; A calendar change took place in the seventeenth century. Therefore, some historical reports of the day state the year as 1642 instead of 1643. But, taking the calendar change into account, the 350th anniversary of the event is correct in the year 1993.

Josephine Morales

2 The Union Man

In my grandfather's living room, hanging on the chimney breast above the black-leaded range, was a large, monotone portrait of a man called Joseph Arch. He was no relation of the family but he played a significant part in the history of our family and, no doubt, in the lives of many a farm labourer in the second half of the nineteenth century.

My great grandfather, William Tanner, was born in 1835. The Tanner family had provided generations of labourers to work on the same local farm at Culkerton in the parish of Rodmarton. Just like his father and grandfather before him, William had worked on the land, first of all as a young lad scaring birds from the crops growing in the fields and then later doing more skilled work. William, however, was not your run-of-the-mill farm labourer. He was literate and when he married Amelia and had a family he saw to it that his

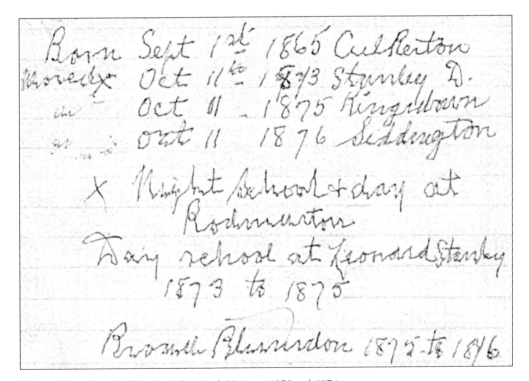

Thomas Tanner's record of the schools he attended between 1873 and 1876.

William and Amelia Tanner on their fiftieth wedding anniversary.

each, read them avidly and relayed the news to his fellow workers. Through those newspapers he learnt of the north/south divide that existed in those days. The north of England in those times was prosperous while farm labourers' wages in Gloucestershire and Wiltshire were very low and only about half the amount paid to farm workers in Lancashire and the northern counties. In 1872 he heard about the newly formed National Union of Agricultural Workers and its leader, Joseph Arch, who was campaigning for improved conditions for farm workers. Probably through the *Labourers' Union Chronicle*, which was established in the same year, William Tanner heard of a proposed meeting to be held at Park Corner in the parish of Duntisbourne Rouse where Joseph Arch would address the local agricultural workers. William's interest was aroused and he was determined to be there and persuaded his friends to join him. What he heard that day convinced him to become a staunch supporter of the National Union of Farm Labourers.

In 1873 William, aware of the poverty suffered by his fellow workers, went to his employer to ask for more wages for himself and the men. He was dismissed. The family lost their home and livelihood. William Tanner, who on census returns always proudly declared himself as a native of Culkerton rather than of the parish of Rodmarton, was the last member of the family to live there. Thus ended over 150 years of occupation by this family who, for generations, had lived, worked and died in the same hamlet. In October 1873 William went to the annual Mop or Hiring Fair in Cirencester, the nineteenth-century equivalent of today's Job Centre, to find employment. No local farmer would hire him. His reputation as a Union man had gone before him. He eventually succeeded in being hired to work on a farm at a place called Stanley Downton near Stonehouse. The wages were low and Amelia had to take in washing to make ends meet but

children went to school in Rodmarton even if it meant making sacrifices from the meagre family earnings to pay the few pence for their education. He knew and recognised the advantages of being able to read and write. In the long winter evenings, when the farm work had been done, the other farm labourers would gather at his cottage and round the kitchen table by the light of oil lamps of candles to learn to read and write. William's children practised their reading and writing skills alongside the other learners. Amelia would join in too for she had been to school in Tetbury.

Although Culkerton may have been the centre of William's universe he was keen to learn about events in the wider world. He regularly bought newspapers for a halfpenny the family had a roof over their head and the children were able to continue their schooling at Leonard Stanley. They stayed there for two years before William went back to the Mop Fair hoping to get work in the Cirencester area. He found that he was still regarded as a troublemaker and no one in or around Cirencester would employ him. The only work offered to him was on a farm at Kingsdown, Wiltshire. The family had a harder time than ever. The cottage was dilapidated, damp and draughty. On a good night when they lay in bed they were able to see the stars through the holes in the roof. On a blustery, rainy night they blocked up the holes and caught the drips as best they could. The family tolerated these conditions for a year. It was better than being in the workhouse and somehow they found enough money for the children to go to school.

The family's luck changed in 1876. In the October of that year William, now aged forty-one years, went back to Cirencester Mop Fair and he was successful in being hired to work at Plummers Farm, Siddington. The family moved into the cottage almost opposite the Greyhound pub. William and Amelia spent the rest of their lives in that cottage. William was employed looking after the horses and then, in his later years, as a gardener. Amelia, with no midwifery qualifications other than her own experience of giving birth and her practical nature, was often called out to help with the birth when her friends and neighbours in the village went into labour.

You could say that William and his wife lived happily ever after. They celebrated their golden wedding in 1907 and when William died aged seventy-nine years in 1915 he had seen many social changes. The conditions for agricultural workers had improved, his grandchildren had benefited from the creation of compulsory state education for children between the ages of five and ten years and he and his wife had benefited from the introduction of a State Pension.

I learnt about William and Amelia from my grandfather, Tom Tanner, as well as through my own research into my family's history. Great-grandfather William and grandfather Tom continued to hold Joseph Arch in great esteem all their lives in spite of the hardships they had endured as man and boy in the cause of working to improve conditions for agricultural workers. The portrait of Joseph Arch was regarded with pride and was never removed from its prime position over the mantelpiece in the living room while Granddad was alive.

Mary Bartlett

3 Memories of the Rajah

Prize-winning entry

Cirencester is well known for its fine Roman heritage and prominence in Roman Britain. Perhaps fewer people realise that at one time the town was associated with the destiny of a family and a unique state of head-hunters extending along the coast of Northern Borneo in South East Asia. Our attention is drawn to Sir Charles Brooke, the second white Rajah, who ruled Sarawak from 1868 to 1917. He epitomised the Brooke policy that 'Sarawak belongs to the Malays, the Sea Dayaks, the Land Dayaks, and the Kayans and other tribes… not to us. It is for them we labour… not for ourselves.'

The three white Rajahs divided their lives between ruling Sarawak in Kuching and taking their leave in England. The town connection does not begin with Rajah James, the first white Rajah. He spent his leave in a small house at Burrator, Sheepstor, in Devonshire. Rajah Charles inherited it and, indeed, spent his honeymoon there. However, his marriage to Margaret Lili de Windt in October 1869 meant that he was now drawn towards the Cotswolds. The home of Margaret, daughter of Clayton de Windt, was Blunsdon Hall, Highworth, in Wiltshire. Charles had no desire to live in London high society which bored him to distraction. He wished to be near his favourite hunting area with the Duke of Beaufort and Ranée, Margaret's friends. The Rajah returned regularly to England in winter for the hunting season. Charles consequently became increasingly attracted to Cirencester and the immediate neighbourhood. He occupied several houses both in and around the town. It would appear that Cecily Hill House could be included among them. At the turn of the century the Rajah became interested in property in Chesterton. His search for an established residence was soon to be fulfilled.

The property he first purchased in the Chesterton district was known as Oakley Villas. He immediately converted it into a well-appointed residence and named it Oakley Hall. He then erected a museum which illustrated the inhabitants, customs, products and natural history of Sarawak. Mr Sheldon, the curator, had to repair the more fragile objects which were damaged from the rough handling the packing cases received en route from the East. The Sarawak Museum was open to the public in October 1901 from 3.00 p.m. to 5.00 p.m. on Tuesdays and Fridays. Gentry who wished to view the items on display at any other time were requested to send their cards the day before stating the hours they wished to call. The most noticeable item on display had been prepared by a London taxidermist. This gigantic python was twenty-one and a half feet long. In the centre of the body was a swelling four feet in diameter and three feet long: just before capture it had bolted down a whole pig live. A boatload of Dayaks had spotted it swimming across the river looking for a quiet spot to digest its prey. The Dayaks gave it a dose of local tobacco, lashed rattans around the monster and delightedly handed it over live to Rajah Charles. The display was regarded as one of the most interesting private collections in the

Sir Charles Anthoni Brooke, 1868-1917, second white Rajah of Sarawak.

Cecily Hill House.

country at that time. However, the collection only remained briefly at Oakley Hall. Chesterton House was advertised for sale in *The Wilts and Gloucestershire Standard* on 8 February. Rajah Charles promptly acquired Chesterton House in 1902 and Oakley Hall was subsequently sold to Lord Grantley. Rajah Charles had now established himself in a spacious and well-furnished residence befitting a wealthy country gentleman of that period.

Rajah Charles erected additional stables and acquired twenty fine hunters. During the hunting season the grooms led them around the district to Earl Bathurst's park for their daily morning exercise. They entered through the Tetbury Road entrance proceeding past the Vale of White Horse kennels down Windsor Walk inside the park. On their return they were dressed and groomed,

remaining in their stables in the afternoon. After each hunt they were given one day's rest. From May to August the Rajah's sleek hunters grazed under the trees in the field beside Fox's Lane. They were thoroughly conditioned ready for his return in early November. Rajah Charles also had a magnificent team of coach horses. His high-steppers were given a daily outing which proved quite an event. He gained a reputation for driving with panache around the countryside and hurtling through the streets of Cirencester. On one occasion he drove straight over Birdlip Hill. On the way down this slope the brakes of the coach refused to work. The Rajah then lashed the wheels together and slid all the way down as best he could. Emma Evelyn, his sister, was inside the coach and she leaned, terrified, out of the window. The Rajah quickly uttered a few comforting words. Emma, a devout

Christian, sat back quietly folding her arms preparing peacefully for the end.

His widowed sister lived at Worcester House on the corner of Chesterton Lane and Somerford Road. She was a well-known figure in the Chesterton district frequently seen being pushed around in a bath chair. Mrs Evelyn mirrored Queen Victoria in appearance, never failing to wear her widow's weeds in public. She was known to distribute religious tracts on every conceivable occasion including missionary leaflets on Sarawak. Gladys informs us that the Rajah's devotion to his younger sister was touching. He never let a day pass without calling on her with 'all the grace and gallantry too often lacking in a frequent visitor.'

The Rajah enjoyed making occasional coaching trips to London with his loyal coachman, Mr Reynolds, who lived in Sheep Street. He wore a distinctive dark green uniform with his huntsman's hat and cockade. They ventured out onto the Bristol to London West Coach Road passing through Fairford, Lechlade, Kingston Bagpuize, Faringdon, Abingdon, Dorchester and Henley. They made two night stops, changing their four horses at Abingdon and Henley, before stabling them on arrival in Islington. They shared the driving though the Rajah worked his horses relentlessly. They usually stayed in London for a fortnight before making the return journey. The Rajah was keen to attend the annual Islington Horse and Coach Show which paraded the latest innovations in coach designs. Presumably Rajah Charles shopped locally at the saddlers, Morris & Harmers, in Cirencester Market Place.

After Lord Grantley had purchased Oakley Hall, Rajah Charles needed a new home for his Sarawak Collection. Therefore he bought a considerable area of land on the other side of Chesterton Lane immediately opposite Chesterton House. On a portion of it near his main gates he had a fine museum and institute built. The design and plans were drawn up by Mr V.A. Lawson and the builder was Mr George Drew who lived in Victoria Road. The front elevation was a picturesque open vestibule similar in design to the old Cirencester Cottage Hospital. The Rajah's motto, Dum Spiro Spero, meaning 'While I breathe, I hope', was on the coat of arms prominently displayed at the front of the building. The Sarawak Collection was now displayed in a spacious, lofty and well-lit room under the care of Mrs Ellen Walker. Visitors walked across the veranda through the main hall and then down a flight of steps to the back of the building. The gigantic python now extended along the entire length of the room, kept company by one of the orangutans holding a metal lamp. Elderly Cirencester residents vividly recalled the Dayak boats and the cases full of butterflies. In the centre of the room was a large display table with a conventional glass cover and various shields, spears, bows and arrows hung around the walls. A recent addition to the original exhibits was a large model of a Dayak dwelling built on piles. Rajah Charles also provided a small reading room and library. The reading room was declared open daily from 10.00 a.m. in October 1904 for the public at large and residents of the Chesterton district in particular. Books could not be taken out or children admitted in the reading room. Smoking was allowed so that visitors could enjoy book and pipe under pleasant conditions. Only one book on Sarawak by Charles Anthony Brooke appears to be listed among the other works in the well-stocked library. Although Sarawak was his passion the Rajah always maintained a keen interest in the old country.

Around the museum and institute Rajah Charles laid out ornamental gardens and pleasure grounds for public use. These included tennis courts, croquet lawns and playgrounds for children. The children could play on the seesaws and stand under the covered shelter when it was raining. The Chesterton children tended to be very possessive of the playground and did not like other children coming up from the town at all. Over the entrance gateway was a lamp which was only lit when the Rajah was in residence. This lamp did not shine during the 1914-1918 war. The whole area was kept in darkness throughout that period. The garden aviary housed specimens of the bird life of Sarawak and other tropical countries including parrots, macaws, cockatoos and game birds such as pheasants. Peacocks also wandered freely around the gardens. They roosted in the trees overlooking Chesterton House on the opposite side of the road and roamed at will around the grounds, frequently wandering back across Chesterton Lane into the museum gardens. They apparently made plenty of raucous noise particularly at night. According to the long-suffering locals this was invariably a sign that it was going to rain.

Cirencester residents in 1985 nostalgically recalled visiting the museum and aviary when they were children. Chesterton was quite rural in those days and there certainly was no transport available in the area. Townspeople simply walked or cycled up from the town usually on Sundays after church. The occasional automobile irritatingly kicked up a lot of swirling dust. The python was vividly remembered and similarly a cockatoo called 'Max'. Mr Max Cole, a local resident who had worked out East, presented it to the Rajah for safekeeping. Every time the children called its name it would come flying over to greet them. The Rajah was particularly fond of children. Occasionally he would take a little boy or girl passing by down to the aviary. He proceeded to take a tiny key from his gold chain, open the door and show the child around the interior. He then collected colourful feathers from the cage floor and handed them to the child as a keepsake. Every year at Whitsun up until the Great War he treated the children of Chesterton to a day

Chesterton House in 1985.

Worcester House in 1985.

out. The boys turned up in their hard-wearing tweed suits, white starched collars and tweed flat caps. The girls wore their best white starched frocks and leather shoes having placed their hair in curlers overnight. Boots were considered boys' footwear in those days. They then scrambled aboard two four-wheeled brakes, seating approximately twenty children, each pulled by two horses. When they were all aboard they gaily trotted off to The George Hotel at Birdlip. On arrival they played games and ran races, eating and drinking as much as they could from the spread laid out on trestle tables. The Rajah similarly organized an annual Christmas party in the museum reading room. They all enjoyed the conventional Christmas festivities and party games. During the summer the children were allowed to pick apples from the orchard near the house.

Rajah Charles further invited the Cirencester brass and reed band to play inside the grounds. This was the Midland Southwestern Works Railway band comprising around thirty members with its headquarters in Watermoor.

It was the established local band prior to the First World War. During the summer they performed on Saturday evenings in the Market Place. On some Sunday afternoons the band performed to the public on the Rajah's lawn directly in front of Chesterton House. They played for one and a half hours completing the performance in time for the Sunday church service at 6.30 p.m. The grounds were also open annually in the same manner as the Querns and Abbey grounds. On these occasions people generally wandered around and admired the gardens.

In October 1916 Rajah Charles fell seriously ill at the Astana in Kuching. The illness started with a swollen ankle which the Rajah dismissed as 'Damned nonsense -and a touch of gout.' The swelling ominously spread from his ankle to his leg. Nevertheless, he amazingly rallied sufficiently to be able to travel home in January 1917. He arrived in mid-February staying initially at Hyde Park Hotel in London. Gladys recalls that he loved to talk about the house at Cirencester hoping that she and Bertram might later live there and

Oakley Hall, Chesterton.

love the old place as he had done. He wished the museum to remain just as he left it when he died. In mid-April he personally requested to be taken to Chesterton House.

He travelled by car to Cirencester accompanied by Doctor Howard Marshall. Ranée Margaret and her two younger sons were in constant attendance. Gladys and Bertram remained at Chesterton House though Vyner had to stay in Colombo to recover from his own serious illness. The Rajah's coughing spells developed into oedema and his heart gradually began to fail. Nevertheless, he continually rallied and seemed to be on the road to recovery when he died quietly at Chesterton House at noon on Thursday 17 May 1917. It was Ascension Day and all the blinds in the house were drawn. Gladys comments that 'All the beauty, gentleness and strength of his nature were revealed upon his face in repose.' He died shortly before his

eighty-eighth birthday. The funeral took place at 2.30 p.m. on Monday 21 May in Cirencester parish church. The family mourners led by Ranée Margaret, Captain Bertram and Gladys Brooke and the Sarawak Officers were seated together on the south side of the nave. The prominent local mourners were headed by Colonel E. Bathurst CMG. The Rajah's coffin was borne by the personal employees of the Rajah at Chesterton House. The clergy and the choir met the coffin at the South Porch and preceded it to the chancel step. The service was simple but impressive and attended by a large congregation. The final prayer before Grace giving thanks for the life and work of the late Rajah had been adapted from the Accession Service. As the coffin left the parish church there was a muffled peal of bells. The mourners followed reverently behind the hearse to London road and then they returned quietly in their carriages to Chesterton

House. Harry Brooke accompanied the hearse to London for the Memorial Service which was held the following Thursday in the chapel of St Michael and St George at St Paul's Cathedral. The general public gathered in enormous crowds outside the small chapel.

The Rajah's body was embalmed and placed in a mausoleum in London awaiting interment in Sarawak. However, contrary to his express wishes, he was buried on 12 June 1919 under the yew tree in the churchyard of Sheepstor beside his uncle, James Brooke, the first white Rajah. The second white Rajah, like the first, lies far away from the country he loved. No more would the white-haired old Rajah be seen dashing in his coach or trap through Cirencester. The periodic coverage of sensational events in Sarawak would soon disappear from the pages of the *Wilts and Gloucestershire Standard*. An association was now ending.

Rajah Charles left Chesterton House, the museum and all it contained to his second son, Bertram. Bertram and Gladys already had a large 200-acre property at Tan Y Garth on the Welsh border. Therefore they decided to rent Chesterton House temporarily as a private boarding school for girls. Subsequently they never lived there as the old Rajah had originally intended, though Emma Evelyn remained in Worcester House for some thirteen years. Since Rajah Vyner never owned Chesterton House, Brooke or Charles Close would appear to be more suitable names for the drive today.

In June 1920 Bertram informed the council that it was not practicable to keep the museum site open for public purposes. The council could not afford to purchase it so the museum remained closed and the aviary was dismantled. All the exhibits were soon taken away by wagon to the railway station. They were last seen piled on the platform presumably London bound though their exact destination remains unknown. They were not stored with the Brooke Collection at the British Museum though Gladys had recently established a London business in the Burlington Arcade. The shop was named 'La Ruche' and she sold useful works of art made by artist craftsmen. It is possible that she gradually sold them off through this new enterprise. The old Rajah's wish that the museum and gardens would continue as they were - open to the public - was not to be. Nevertheless, in his time Rajah Charles had formed a close association with Cirencester and had deep affection for Chesterton House. It remains an historically significant building to this day.

Michael B. Clarke

4 Oxen in the Park

Prize-winning entry

Before the First Earl Bathurst began to enclose the sheep runs round Cirencester town, the whole of the Cotswolds were open and unfenced so that the extensive use of oxen in this part of Gloucestershire can only date from the early eighteenth-century. Thus it was that the oxen owed their existence to this great family which can trace its history back to Saxon times and they could have had no more picturesque setting in all these Cotswold hills than this fine old park of Cirencester. Having spent all my working life in the Park I have come to know and love it and yet have never tired of the lovely surroundings, even after my excursions with the oxen to the romance and interest of the film studios, and I have always been rather glad to leave all the noise and bustle behind me and get back to the green quiet of the woods and fields again, even though it meant more hard work and the end of my holiday.

The Park itself was largely laid out by the First Earl, Lord Allen Bathurst, and the poet Pope, and together they planned out all the lovely woods and avenues that are today open to the townsfolk of Cirencester – a rare privilege that has not been granted by many other great landowners. The estate is one of the largest in England and although some of the trees have been cut down during two World Wars it is still a place of great charm and beauty and a real paradise for the

The Broad Ride, Cirencester Park.

Hay making in Cirencester Park.

huntsman who can follow the hounds all day without ever leaving the confines of the Park.

I suppose that the best view of the Park can be seen from the old parish church of St John Baptist which is situated in the middle of the town facing the market square. By signing the register and paying a small fee, one can climb to the top of the tower and, looking westwards, there is a marvellous view of the Park and its woods as they stretch out towards the Duke of Beaufort's Estate and the head of the Golden Valley.

Nearer at hand can be seen Cirencester House, for over two centuries the stately home of the Bathurst family and although it almost stands in the streets of the town it is quite hidden from view by the famous yew hedge that is claimed to be the highest in England, and even in the world, the yews rising up for nearly forty feet so that it is known to be a skilled job to clip and trim them. The house, which was rebuilt by the First Lord Bathurst from an Elizabethan mansion called Oakley Grove, is said to have as many windows as there are days in the year,

that is to say 365, and from the town side it is approached through a narrow gateway of freestone. From its portal, in the year 1943, the Late Earl Bathurst, the seventh in the line, was borne to the quiet shade of the old church on a farm wagon that was drawn by the ox, Blossom. I felt honoured to be the ox-attendant and so to pay my last tribute to him, a very grand old gentleman for whom I had the greatest respect and reverence.

Behind the house can be seen the Broad Avenue, a grassy ride which reaches as far as seven miles away, and whose turf I have often rolled with my ox-team. From the Cecily Hill Park Gates in Cirencester town above the old Militia Barracks, the avenue leads on between the tall beech trees to the stone bower called Pope's Seat, where the famous poet used to sit and admire the view and draw inspiration from the beautiful surroundings. Nearby is the junction of seven drives down which one could see in the days before the woods grew up, the church towers of Cirencester, Coates, Kemble and the statue of Queen Anne. Beyond, one goes past the polo fields and the

Ploughing in Cirencester Park, c. 1920.

Water Splash (a sort of old quarry) by the Horse Guards, where stand a couple of stone sentry boxes like those to be seen in Whitehall, and so on to the Ten Rides in Oakley Wood where ten avenues all lead out from a central point to different corners of the Park, each of them a grassy track beloved of horseman and horsewoman. Not far from this junction and near to the Five Mile Lodge on the road from Stroud to Cirencester is a stone building that is known as 'Alfred's Hall', but although the site is supposed to have some connection with the old king of that name, and the ruin has sometimes deceived the antiquarians, it is really one of those 'Follys' that were once so popular with great landowners and was built during the eighteenth century.

On the left of the Broad Avenue is the Old Deer Park where a famous herd was once kept and this part of the park was also well known as a camping ground for the Army for more than a century. Here one stands in the middle of the Park against the high statue of Queen Anne which was erected to her memory by the First Earl Bathurst, and looking towards the town there is a fine view of the house with the parish church in the background. In the past it was a wonderful sight to see the deer and cattle grazing together with a pack of hounds taking their daily exercise nearby and all these different animals just not taking any notice of each other.

The Park was well known for its good grazing and I have often taken good fat prime cattle to market from it. During the summer we also turned out our ox-teams to graze there and when bringing them in at the beginning of a day's work we usually got our feet and legs very wet, for the grass was long, and on reaching the farm we would take our boots off and empty the water out. The long grass was also a good cover for the young fawns; often times we had fun trying to catch one but they were always too quick for us.

When the horse chestnuts were ripe and falling we boys were paid so much to collect them, after which they were put in store and given to the deer after the weather began to get hard. Even today there are still a few deer in the park, though of a rather wild nature and they can be seen occasionally in the woods of Hailey, Oakley and Overley, often visited during the springtime for their picturesque carpets of bluebells and primroses, colourful beneath the tall larch and beech trees.

During the Second World War the Park was taken over to build a large American Hospital and the huts remain there today, but on the boundary is a site of a much earlier military activity, for at a spinney called the Rifle Butts the militia used to stand their targets and oftentimes as boys we have dug around the loose earth and found the old lead bullets, long since forgotten. All through its long history the Park has had close military associations and perhaps the climax came in 1944 when the headquarters transports of Montgomery and Eisenhower were quartered in the Avenue.

Keeping to the Avenue between Pope's Seat and the Horse Guards one passes through the Rough Hills where the Forestry gardens are situated and here the young trees are tended until they are strong enough to take their place in the large woods. I have spent some exciting days on these hills and during the haymaking we had to be very careful as this is where our worst enemy, the adder, is to be found. The adder is easy to distinguish from the ordinary grass snake for it is brown in colour with a black V-mark on its head and has a black stripe right down the centre; the end of its tail is rounded whereas that of a grass snake runs down to a point. Until quite recently the Head Forester would pay four pence for each adder that was killed and since when danger is near an adder will swallow her young for protection, if you were lucky enough to kill one of these you would claim four pence for each little one as well.

During the hay operations it was often very hot, and one such day I was asked to fetch some cider from the farm manager's house. On my way back with a large stone jar I began to feel thirsty and lodging the jar on a low wall I had a good drink from it. Feeling well satisfied with myself I started off again amidst roars of laughter for my struggling with the jar on the wall was witnessed by a picnic party whose presence I had not noticed. Where we used to make hay on these hills in the days of my boyhood are now self-planted oak trees and shrubs and in the future this part of the park may well be classed as woodland. There is one plantation called the Jubilee plantation with fine larches growing to a height of twenty feet, and during the First World War I helped to plough this plot of land many times with the faithful old ox team; each time I pass by these odd spots it brings back memories of my boyhood days as an ox lad.

Continuing on through the Park along the Broad Avenue one approaches the village of Sapperton, built on the hillside overlooking the Golden Valley and there is a pleasant scene towards the church steeple of Bisley nearly three miles away. Sapperton has its own little church and near it runs the old railway tunnel, one of the longest in England, and also the old canal tunnel.

My grandfather on my mother's side was a barge master on the Thames and Severn Canal and when he took his barge from Cirencester Wharf down to Stroud he was forced to 'leg' his way through. The bargees used to lie on their backs on the bow deck and work their feet on the sides of the tunnel to keep the barge going, and while they made the two-and-a-half mile journey underground the donkeys would be taken along the path through Hailey Wood to take over at the other end.

From the Thames at Lechlade the old canal wound past many a Cotswold village to the head of the Golden Valley at Daneway where it dropped down to Stroud by a good many locks, and there the Stroudwater Navigation carried on to the Severn Estuary at Framilode. I believe that some of the barges used to get on to the Gloucester Canal near there and trade up towards the Midlands. Below Chalford there is water in it yet, but between Sapperton and the Thames most of the bed is now dry and grass-grown and even the old three-storeyed inn, the Tunnel House where the bargees used to refresh themselves before undertaking their subterranean journey, was gutted by fire. All this is a sad change from the days of 1788 when no less a person than George III himself came to Cirencester House and afterwards drove through the Park to look at the work then in progress on the canal, in which the Lord Bathurst of that time was an interested shareholder. Even as I write these words the local press has announced that the last part of this Thames-Severn water route, the little Stroudwater Canal, is to be closed and so the last chapter of these Gloucestershire waterways has quietly drawn to its close.

I think that the last barge went through the Sapperton Tunnel about three or four years before the First World War and was laid up at Siddington, but it was long after that when the canal was finally abandoned, and for many years it lay there weedy and desolate with the locks falling into ruin and the brickwork of the bridges slowly crumbling away. Now the farmers have put barbed wire and fencing posts across the bed and only the old folk remember having seen a barge in these parts. A branch of the canal came up to the wharf in Cirencester town, but that too has long been derelict and the days when my grandfather's barge came up that way are gone forever, like the old man himself.

Many times when out at work with my team I have seen the oxen prick their ears forward and have heard the baying of dogs in the far-off distance. Soon has come the sound of the huntsman's horn mingled with the cry

Oxen and hounds.

of the hounds as they begin to get nearer and then the fox would break cover and come sneaking through the hedge. Perhaps he would cross our furrows and we would stop our ploughs to avoid breaking the line of scent. As he steals across the field to the nearest spinney to be out of sight of the chase the hounds are now very near and they stop at the hedgerow and hesitate. We point to the line of the fox and the direction he has taken and the huntsman encourages his pack to get going. Once again they pick up the scent and in a moment they are gone, with the excited followers, spread out across the field, some with their scarlet coats, the gentlemen with their top hats gleaming in the sun and the ladies in their traditional bowlers, and the horses enjoying the sport every bit as much as their masters and mistresses, doing their utmost so that their riders shall be there at the kill. Often Master Renard eludes them and the hounds pick up the scent of another fox

and then they can be heard pacing through the woods until they make their kill or the scent fails again and they lose it altogether.

This part of Gloucestershire has long been famous as a hunting centre and when Lord Bathurst's hounds are in full cry across the Park it is a fine sight indeed and one that might have been witnessed at any time during the last hundred years or so since the kennels on the Fosse Way were built by the fourth Earl. A good horse and a good seat are essential in this district for although one can hunt all day in the 3,000 acres of the Park without ever leaving it, the ground is well varied with hills, valleys and coverts and open grass and plough land, and the short sharp rises can be very exacting to both horse and rider.

Apart from Lord Bathurst's hounds a good many other famous packs have hunted around the Cotswolds during the past century, and the V.W.H, (Vale of White Horse) hounds, the

Cotswold hounds, and the Duke of Beaufort's Badminton Pack are all well-known in these parts.

A day's sport that I have often enjoyed is acting as a beater for the deer stalkers, and although it means a considerable amount of walking and one is very tired at the end of the day it is a fascinating and worthwhile pastime, especially if one gets a share of the spoils. The deer have a great sense of smell so it is highly probable that when the beaters line up at the edge of a large woodland they will be already scented unless they have taken good care to move up against the wind. The guns are already lined up a mile or so away and often during the drive one does not see any deer at all, though one can see where they have been, until the crack of the guns rings out and then you know that there are some about.

The deer flesh or venison is very rich and because there is very little fat attached to it a really good cook is needed to make the meat at all palatable. During the mating season the deer are dangerous to approach, and when the fawns are born during the months of May and June the doe usually hides them away from human view in the daytime in the middle of a bunch of nettles or bracken.

Pheasant beating is very similar to deer stalking for the birds are driven out of the coverts by a line of beaters made up of men and boys and the guns shoot whilst the birds are in full flight; occasionally we would set up a hare as well and he would run to meet his doom as he got within range of the guns. Though pheasants are considered to be good sporting birds they are quite stupid when roosting and can easily be taken from the lower branches of a tree at night by a good many means. Some of the poachers in days gone by used to use a mere pinch of shot and powder in an old muzzle-loading gun whilst others would blind them with a light and then fetch them down with a stick or smoke the

Jimmy and Joey.

Tarzan comes to Cirencester. A film promotion of 1938.

birds insensible with sulphur fumes as did the bargees in Hailey Wood.

Perhaps the best sporting day of all for the farm hand was during the rabbit shooting for it was always active and eventful since the rabbits often turn back when they get within range of the guns and try to get between the beaters and we were kept busy all the time with never a dull moment. Though perhaps these sports are not so exciting for the beater as for the man with the gun, they always made a welcome change from the everyday routine of farm work even if the sport had been particularly good, we could always trek to the wayside inn during the lunch break to enjoy a quiet glass of beer with our sandwiches and talk over the day's sport.

Travelling round the country lanes of Gloucestershire or working in the fields, it is just part of the everyday sights of our life to see the rabbits hopping and scurrying along the hedgerow or jumping out of a tuffet of grass.

Though some farmers declare rabbits to be nothing more than a pest these animals helped to solve our meat problem during the war, and although they may be classed as vermin they can hardly be compared with rats, for the latter have no sentimental place in our imagination and are of no value as food, often infesting buildings and spreading disease which rabbits have never done. As they are the victims of so many foes already it is very sad to see them die of myxamatosis and if men spread the disease for their destruction then in my opinion they should be severely penalised; once you have seen them in this pitiful state it takes a long time before you can relish eating one again.

If the foes of the rabbit – such as the stoat, a nasty little animal that has a habit of picking out the best before chasing them to their death – are deprived of their natural food then the farmer may well suffer as a consequence and it might well be that the foxes will in time descend in numbers like the wolves of old to attack the poultry and even the young lambs.

On this large estate rabbits have never become a real problem, perhaps because the workers have been allowed to take them when they could and so the animals have been kept in check. It is, I think, a queer state of affairs that most of the farmers who complain about the number of rabbits on their land would soon clap hands on anyone they caught there with a rabbit on him and would haul him up before the local magistrates as a poacher, whilst if he asked permission to catch the rabbits he would almost certainly be refused and told to go elsewhere.

Apart from the 'blood sports' the Park is also noted for its polo and the Cirencester Club has spent the last four years in bringing the game back to the pre-war standard. Between the two wars the polo played here was first class and before the Army was mechanised they could field some really good teams which were a delight to watch, but during the last war the fields were ploughed up and grew some remarkably fine crops. Today three grand playing fields are again in use and a feature is the Pavilion Clock which

was recently noted in the press as the only one of its kind in the country, being invented by a local man and so arranged that it registers the length of a chukka. This is a great help to the players for when a match is in progress they can tell at a glance how much time they have left in which to win or lose.

Many of England's best polo players have visited the Park and one can always be sure of seeing some good horsemanship, the Hon. George Bathurst, the Earl's younger brother was an enthusiastic rider. It is remarkable how the ladies have now taken to the sport and just in the Cirencester Park Polo Tournament four ladies played against four gentlemen and ended up the victors by four to one, Mr Jimmy Edwards the well known radio comedian being one of the losers.

In the old days horses were used to prepare the field for playing and I have often given a helping hand with my ox team on the 30 cwt. roller, but here again the tractors have come into the picture and most of the work is now done with their aid, leaving little for my two remaining oxen. In the days when the Indian Princes came to play polo they were very

Ralph, son of Edward Smith, leading Cirencester Carnival in 1932.

33

Cirencester Carnival, c. 1930.

interested in our methods of farming with the oxen and it seemed strange to us country lads to hear their grooms talking in their foreign tongue as they passed us at work in the fields.

As you stand watching the Polo you can see in the background some old cottages with battlements on the top, called the Ivy Lodge, the Square House, the Round House, and the Pike House, and although their full history is unknown to me I know a little about two of them. The Pike House goes back to the days when there used to be a public road running straight through the Park to the West Country for it is where the old coaches used to stop for refreshments and the cellar and the huge stone block on which the barrels stood can still be seen, whilst in the door is the little round hole through which the keeper used to peep before opening up. When one of the Earl Bathursts decided to make the Park a private one, the present Stroud Road which runs round the boundary of the Estate was built and the coach road through the Park was then closed.

The Round House, which is similar to the toil-cottages on the Thames and Severn Canal must also be of a good age and its walls are a good yard thick with very small windows. I spent the first fifteen years of my married life there and although it was pleasant enough in the summer it was very quiet and isolated in the winter time and like most other places in the Park it brought back memories of my boyhood.

When I was an ox-lad to the head ox-man on one very cold winter's morning with the snow falling heavily all round us he told me his wife wanted me and going round to the cottage she asked me to watch over the two children while she went to town to buy some provisions, this being my job for the rest of that day. In later years when sitting by that same fireplace with my own two children I could not help but think that I was living that morning of many winters ago all over again and that life in my small world was full of coincidences.

The cottage which I now occupy was erected in 1924 and built with the compass on land which I have many times helped to plough and cultivate with my six-ox team. It has six large rooms with four south windows, one west window and two north windows, very solidly built of Cotswold stone with a good sized vegetable garden and it is now in the course of being fully modernized.

From the threshold of my cottage I can often hear the church bells of Daglingworth calling the parishioners to worship, and when they are ringing they usually sound as though they are saying 'Ding, dong, puff' and from this the local nickname for Daglingworth is 'Daddy-puff.'

Set on the hillside about two miles away the little Saxon and Roman church overlooks the stream and village and the old smithy, snugly and prettily hidden away from any approach by road. The neighourhood is well known for its Dag stones, a very hard type of stone that is often used for rockeries and as the seam reaches to some of our outlying fields it is rather a menace to us for when out cultivating it has caused a great number of breakages to our implements. From these stones the village has taken its name of course, and from the farm which had the last ox-team there we bought the ox-harness and it hangs in our stable to this day still in good condition but once again almost unwanted.

Though much has changed in the district since I was born in Gloucester Street, on the west side of Cirencester, and the recent increase in population has caused many new housing estates to be built, there are still many fine buildings to be seen and the old town is much to be admired.

From its Roman origin the town is sometimes called 'Ciceter', but more often than not the local inhabitants say simply 'Ciren'. It stands at the junction of a number of Roman roads, amongst them being the Fosse Way and the Ermin and Akeman Streets and whether one takes the roads to Gloucester, Swindon, Tetbury or Stow they are all remarkably straight and free from bends. Many Roman remains have been found in the district but there must surely be many more than have not yet been unearthed, and as I write these words I know of an old stone coffin the foot of which is just protruding from the ground.

Not the least interesting of the buildings is the old parish church and my brother Sidney, who held office as verger there for many years, once wrote a book about it, a copy of which is still in my possession, but to tell of its history, and that of the Abbey, the wool trade, the Roman Amphitheatre, and a host of other things would take several books, and though I shall have something to say in a later chapter about the town's historical Mop Fair I must content myself here by saying that the Cirencester of today can still merit, as it always has done, its time honoured title, 'The Capital of the Cotswolds.'

Edward Charles Smith

5 School Days

A child's history of Chesterton Primary School

I have recently left Chesterton Primary School, as I start at Deer Park School in September, but, while I was there, I wondered how it came to be there. Well, I now have the answer and I will share it with everyone else. Most people think of history as being about events that occurred long ago. The school is only about thirty years old, but it still has a history. None of the current pupils were even thought of then and some of their parents may not have been born.

Chesterton is on the outskirts of Cirencester. The town has very distant origins, going back to pre-Roman times. Cirencester is actually best known for its Roman history, having been Corinium, the capital of Roman England. The town, as we see it today, was developed from the medieval era, through to Victorian times, and into the twentieth century.

The six acres of school grounds were once part of the grounds of Chesterton House, which is still there today. The house was owned by a number of people, including the White Rajah of Sarawak, who owned it from 1913. His real name was Charles Brooke and he died in 1917. Then the house was passed on to Vyner Brooke, Charles' first son. Later, ownership was passed to his brother, Bertram Brooke. He owned the house until 1925.

In the years immediately before the school was built, the site was largely occupied by some allotments, where local people grew flowers and vegetables.

The contract to build the school was agreed on the 23 April 1970. Then the builders, Orchard & Peer from Stroud, came in. The school would have eight classrooms, with infants and juniors in the same building. It cost £83,884 and took thirty-three weeks to build.

The official opening of the school was on Tuesday 26 April 1972 at 2.15 p.m. The official guests invited to the opening included the architects, other local headmasters, education officials, school managers and the headmaster's wife. The school was opened by Alderman Lt-Col. S.R.M. Jenkins, MC, the Chairman of the Gloucestershire Education Committee.

When the school opened, there were only eighteen staff. The headmaster was Mr Morris Harding, formerly head at Millbourne Port Junior School in Somerset. There were six teaching staff. Three of them came from Lewis Lane Infant School Annexe in Apsley Road: Miss P. Durham, Mrs J. Lewis and Miss E. Roberts. The other three were Miss A. Symons, Mrs L. Lewis and Mr D. Buck; one from Powells School, one from Fairford and the other from Gloucester. The other staff were a half-time welfare assistant, a supervisory assistant, a part-time secretary, a part-time cleaner, a caretaker, a cook supervisor, an assistant cook and four canteen assistants. Later, other teaching staff joined the school. Among those remembered by early students were Miss Osmond, Mrs De Clifford, Mr Walsh, Miss Hill, Mr Allen and Mr Ratcliffe.

The school began with 194 on the roll. There were forty-eight from Powells School, four from Watermoor School, thirty-eight from Lewis Lane Junior School and seven from Lewis Lane Infant School. To begin with there were six classes, one for each year group.

In 1997, the school's new infant block was opened. It was opened by Gloucestershire's Director of Education and later visited by Princess Anne (the Princess Royal). During 1999/2000, a new classroom was added. Also during 2000, a number of pupils were featured in a programme on BBC Radio 4.

Since the opening, the school has changed a great deal. The numbers have increased; there are now approximately 300 pupils, about 120 Infants and 180 Juniors. There are thirteen classrooms, ten of which are class-based. There are forty staff: the headmaster, the deputy head, eleven teachers, eight support staff and nineteen other staff. There are modern facilities, like televisions and computers, all over the school. Also, there is an Information and Communications Technology (ICT) suite, with a state-of-the-art interactive whiteboard. Another modern facility is the drama studio, equipped with microphones and spotlights. Within the grounds of the school is the Specific Learning Difficulties (SpLD) Centre, for pupils with learning difficulties such as dyslexia. The centre is used by one or two Chesterton pupils and it is also frequently attended by children from other local schools.

The canteen food is no longer cooked at the school. It is delivered to the school and served by one person, usually helped by one or two dinner ladies. However, the majority of students bring packed lunches. For children whose parents work hours before and/or after school, there is the Busy Bees club, which is open from 7.45 a.m. and closes at 5.45 p.m. There are plenty of things for the children to do and there are special activities during the holidays.

Under the watchful eye of the present headmaster, Howard Gray (who very helpfully contributed material for this article), Chesterton Primary School is well prepared to face the challenges of the twenty-first century. You can read all the latest news at the school's own Web site: http://atschool.eduweb.co.uk/chesterton.

Emmeline Walls (age eleven)

The oldest schoole?

A town the size of Roman Corinium must have had schools and colleges of some description. Similarly the various conquerors who followed the Roman withdrawal must have had educational establishments, particularly of an ecclesiastical character. By the time of the Norman Conquest, the town of Cirecestre, as Domesday spells it, surely must have had one or two. Regrettably, details have not come down to us.

Henry VIII has a lot to answer for. The abolition of the monasteries in 1439 including the Abbey of St Mary, resulted in the loss of documentation which might have enabled us more thoroughly to research the early history of the town's 'oldest' school. The loss of those primary sources meant that historians have had to search amongst the few ancient documents that survive to gain a glimpse into what 'education' was like in the Middle Ages.

There are documents suggesting that some form of school, apart from those connected with the Abbey, was in existence in Cirencester as early as 1242. One gives the name of John Brownyng as being a headmaster in 1346. The earliest reliable documents, in 1457 and 1458, speak of John Chedworth, Bishop of Lincoln, endowing a school with £10 per annum as salary for a schoolmaster. However, it is not clear whether he was endowing an existing school or creating a new one. About half a century later Thomas Ruthal, Bishop of Durham, who had been educated at the school, made further endowments. Exactly where this school was is not clear. One suggestion was that it might have been in church property and another that it was on a site in Dyer Street near to where the Bear Inn stands. By 1548 the school had moved to permanent premises in Park Lane. The actual building, much altered but recognisable, still exists and has thrown up many artefacts showing an occupation of the site since Roman times. It gives us the first certain chronological and geographical points of reference. Pupillage there was an all-male affair with about 100 boys being taught in rather cramped conditions in the single hall during 1570. The basic qualification then seems to have been the ability to read the 'Englishe Testament' and pay twelve pence if the 'sonne of a townesman' and three shillings if the son of an 'out dweller'. What of the fair sex? By a statute of the Stuart period it was confirmed that 'noe woemen chieldren bee admytted'.

In the early days the concept of local education appears to have consisted of a passing on of knowledge to the younger generation, especially males, in the hope that the newly acquired information would be used in the furtherance of trade and commerce in the area. In the 'grammar schools' things were different, the accent being on subjects such as Latin, Greek and Rhetoric thus pointing those pupils' careers in specific directions. As the years progressed, certainly by the seventeenth and eighteenth centuries, that vision seems to have been modified in the sense that really outstanding pupils were seen as also having the potential to play a part in research, particularly in scientific fields. As far as the 'old' Grammar School was concerned this reached its climax in the mid 1700s. The headmaster of the time was John Washbourn and amongst his pupils was Edward Jenner of smallpox vaccination fame. He is credited with saving more human lives than anyone else in history. There was also a handful of his contemporaries at the school who were similarly destined to become famous in the world of science.

Others found their fortune in the City and in 1749 the Cirencester Society in London purchased a clock which they presented to the school. The clock still ticks away merrily today having had a place of honour at Park Lane and at later premises used by the school.

Headmasters of the old Grammar School in Park Lane were a mixed bunch in many ways. Most were academically well-qualified although the ability to pass on their knowledge was not always evident. The pupils of Thomas Helmes were said to 'have not much proffited under him'. When he was sacked in 1583 he stubbornly remained on at the school for some time teaching his charges with his usual 'unskillfulness and slackness'. Henry Topp had the misfortune to be head at the time of the Civil War. When the town was taken by Prince Rupert in 1643 he fled to London but later returned and was restored to his post by the Royalists. Unfortunately for him, by the late 1640s, the Parliamentary forces had taken control of the county and he was ordered to leave. In the 1780s John Washbourn clashed with the Vestry, effectively his employers, abandoned all attempts to keep the school open and dismissed his boarders. He continued to live on in the premises, scholarless, until his death about twenty years later. In 1861 William Bartram punished a boy for trespassing on adjoining premises to retrieve a ball. He was taken to court by the boy's father. The court held that a schoolmaster, being *in loco parentis*, had the same rights as parents and declared a box on the ears to be 'the good old English mode of punishment'.

During the nineteenth century it becomes clear that the 'grammar' syllabus was gradually being added to by subjects from the arts and sciences. More accent was placed on preparation for business life and for the entrance examinations to universities and medical establishments. By 1868 the Endowed Schools Commission described the establishment as 'a second class, semi-classical school of fairly successful character'. In the 1870s moves were made to re-site the school on a larger scale in purpose-built premises at New Road, later to be renamed Victoria Road.

This opened in 1881, the first roll call producing only nine boys although there were more on the books. This was typical of Park Lane times where the numbers of pupils reported had always fluctuated wildly. For example, in 1829 there were thirty-two on the roll of whom twenty-two boarded at the school, and in 1835 between fifty and sixty of whom twenty lived on the premises. In 1900 the number rose during the year from fifteen to eighty-five. Possibly the totals recorded depended upon the time of year being referred to in a particular document. Initially the school consisted of the main buildings incorporating the assembly hall which still fronts Victoria Road. In the early 1900s technical classes were held during the evenings, the school thus having a dual purpose for a short period in its history. Over the years separate entrances for the boys and girls came about and further classrooms and laboratories were added at the rear on one side. A two-storey set of classroom buildings was erected on the other side to house the girls when they became equal scholars with the boys.

Pre-twentieth century girls, it seems, if they were from a privileged background, originally relied on tutors, either on a one-to-one basis or in small groups. Their undoubted right to a more scholastic training was sadly neglected until the 1870 Education Act. In Cirencester a girls 'High School' was set up in The Avenue in 1901. But, because the premises were not entirely suitable, they found themselves invited to join the boys in Victoria Road. Well, not quite 'join' the boys. For the first forty years, at least, the two sexes were required to walk to school separately, although brothers and sisters were exempted and could walk together if they chose. At school they used separate entrances, were taught separately and during breaks shared a playground divided by an eight foot high oak fence! After their admission in 1904 the number of pupils rose to 180. At the same time 30 pupils (probably all boys) were boarded at premises in The Avenue vacated by the girls' High School.

The effect of two world wars on the school was marked. Old Boys and Girls donned the uniforms of the HM Forces, many were decorated, some wounded. Others, some thity-six men in the First World War and thirty-nine in the Second World War, lost their lives and are commemorated on memorials now in the Bingham Hall. In the First World War records show that the wounded were quickly patched up to fight again. There were a number of instances in which soldiers were treated, sent back to the front line and wounded a second time, within a matter of days.

The other effects of the wars on the school were quite different. In the First World War, by 1915, many masters joined up leaving the school short of staff. Thus, while the pupil numbers remained about the same, the staff available to teach them fell alarmingly. This was largely overcome by masters working in class almost without a break and the employment of mistresses to teach the boys as well as the girls. At that time there were 190 pupils but by the end of hostilities, the number had risen to 300 in 1920, necessitating the construction of a corridor of allegedly temporary wooden classrooms out of sight behind the main buildings. The major effect of the Second World War came about as a result of the wholesale evacuation of children from areas in the south east thought to be at risk. The number of pupils almost doubled to over 600 at times during the period 1939 to 1945. The pupil/staff ratio problems were less marked in the sense that about the same number of staff taught classes, although these were now double their previous size. Another factor was that several of the masters who had served in the Fist World War were now beyond call-up age and taught throughout the second conflict. The use of mistresses during the Second World War to make up any shortfall was not seen as such a big deal as it had been earlier.

There is little evidence that sporting activities played an important part in the curriculum before the school moved to the Victoria Road premises. In the early days there were no proper sports facilities. Games periods often meant a trek from Park Lane or Victoria Road to Cirencester Park carrying the equipment - goal posts and all. However, shortly before the Great War, the sports field at the rear of the school was purchased with the result that fine facilities became available with cricket and football becoming extremely popular. With the encouragement of Mr Thomas Frazer, the headmaster from 1915 to his death in 1945, cricket was in the ascendancy, the school producing stalwarts in county cricket in the form of Messrs Hammond, Neale and Witchell who dominated county cricket in the 1920s and 1930s. Walter Hammond, holder of the school batting record with an innings of 365 and, by then, an established Test cricketer, was dismissed (caught and bowled) for a duck in an Old Boys match against the School in 1931 by one of the masters. For some reason rugby football never took off as it seems to have done in other Gloucestershire grammar schools. This may have been merely a reflection of the abilities and preferences of the staff. An interest in rugby only emerged after 1945 when Major Peter Gedge was appointed to the headship. Major Gedge was a former trialist for the England rugby team so, not surprisingly, a strange shaped ball soon appeared on the premises which boys could lawfully pick up and run with. By contrast girls' tennis, hockey and netball was played to a high standard

throughout the period at Victoria Road.

Thomas Frazer is probably the best remembered headmaster. He joined the school in 1908, became head in 1916 and served until his death in 1945. He saw the school through difficult periods in two world wars and encouraged all manner of sporting and extra curricular activities. A no-nonsense man, he used the cane frequently with the result that discipline amongst the boys was normally very good, if not they took good care not to be found out. For the few who were caught, in most cases the fear of waiting outside the head's office was the punishment while the subsequent well-deserved 'six of the best' came as a relief.

In 1958, tracing its origins from the 1458 endowment, celebrated its quincentenary. It was not until 1966 that the end finally came. A decision was made to amalgamate the Grammar School and other local schools on the now completed Deer Park complex to form a comprehensive school. And so it is that education in Cirencester can be traced as far back as 1242 and with certainty from 1458. One school, the town's grammar, formed the basis of education in town for at least five centuries. For the last four decades it has been joined with 'younger' establishments such as Powells, Lewis Lane and others, all now part of a successful comprehensive system centred on the Deer Park complex.

Incidentally, the premises in Victoria Road are still a school, occupied now by the County Infants School and County Junior School. Those lucky boys and girls occupy a building with a proud history extending over a period of eighty-five years. So, in a way, 'the old schoole is alive and well. It can trace its history from the era of the wool trade to the world of the information highway. May good fortune follow its successor at the Deer Park.

Peter Rowe

Bibliography

The History of Cirencester and the Roman City of Corinium, Kennet Beecham (1886).

The Cirencestrian school magazine 1919-1966, especially articles by Kennet Beecham,

The History of Cirencester Grammar School (incorporating a dissertation, *A History of the First Cotswold Grammar School 1241-1966* by John Ireland BA) compiled and edited by Edwin Cuss (1993).

Looking back at Cirencester Grammar School, Edwin Cuss (1996).

School on the move

For fifty-six years, Querns School has been part of the Cirencester scene. Its gracious frontage on Querns Lane conceals approximately two acres of garden behind which stretches as far as Paternoster House and the Council Offices. The grounds overlie part of the Roman town of Corinium; excavations have revealed a mosaic floor, a well, coins and pottery fragments dating from the fourth century. The school had its origin in Cirencester Grammar School. After the 1944 Education Act, the Grammar School needed to expand and the Kindergarten department needed to move. Their first home was in the Masonic Hall.

In 1946, Miss Kathleen Goodworth, who was in charge of the kindergarten department, and her sister, Winifred, purchased Querns Lane House. The school was opened on Thursday 19 September 1946. Miss Goodworth kept detailed records of the children and events at the school in her small two shilling notebook for the thirteen years she was headmistress. She also kept notes of old pupils and their success at university, marriages, births and even a poignant memorial of pupils who had died – mostly in accidents.

Children at the school were prepared for the Eleven Plus and Common Entrance exams; most children acquiring places at the Grammar School or other schools of their choice. The school took an active part in local events, raised

Mrs Paine and Form II on the way to London 1961.

Querns School, c. 1955.

The Pencil Fence, 1998.

money for various charities and battled with outbreaks of whooping cough, measles, mumps and chicken pox.

There were two inspections, in 1950 and 1957, both commending the school for its education and secure, happy, caring environment. Miss Goodworth and her sister retired in 1959. On 24 April the Misses Goodworth gave a leaving party for the children and staff in the church hall (in Lewis Lane where Akeman Court now stands). They were presented with a standard lamp, a Parker Knoll chair and two boxes of chocolates – and everybody was entertained by a conjuror.

Mr Walters was headmaster from 1959 until 1985. He created a school uniform for the children complete with ties, school coats, hats and caps. He also had the swimming pool installed which has been used extensively in the summer until the present day (though the water is now heated). Mr Walters also established formal games lessons and matches were played against other schools. He followed cricket test matches avidly. He continued to prepare the children for examinations and proved himself to be a superb and fascinating history teacher. Mr Walters also started the annual cake competition which has lasted until now.

Outings from the school happened regularly. Mr Walters retired in 1985 and the school was taken over by one of his daughters, Jane Peters, who, together with her husband Robert, were principals until 2002. The school building was altered internally; the living quarters were moved to the rear wing and the school occupied the road-side section on three floors. A school hall was now required. Money was raised and the hall was completed in 1988 – three heads attended the ceremony, Miss Goodworth, Mr Walters and Mrs Paine.

Mrs Muriel Paine became headmistress in 1985. She joined the school in 1954 to teach the top class and taught until her retirement in 1998 - a total of forty-four years service. She kept a scrapbook of information and cuttings

Miss Goodworth's notebook, 1946.

from the *Standard* which are a delight to read.

The school continued to thrive under Mrs Paine's dedicated and expert guidance. It took an active part in the local community – sports, small schools swimming galas, country dance festivals and also the BBC Television broadcast of *Songs of Praise* at the parish church. The school raised money for national and international charities with various activities The old folks of Querns Lane Flats, Akeman Court and the almshouses were the lucky recipients of log cakes each Christmas - (one old lady even knocked at a school window demanding her cake!).

Mr Ian Culley became head in 1998 bringing with him After School Activities and the colourful 'pencil fence'. Two years later, Mr Chris Whytehead arrived as the head. The school continued to flourish and exam results were excellent. In January 2002 came the unexpected but exciting news that the school was to move to Westonbirt, near Tetbury, where it will benefit from extensive grounds, sports facilities including an indoor swimming pool, music rooms, science laboratories and more computers.

In July 2002 the children from Querns were given a party to mark the end of their time in Querns, Cirencester – this time it was a barbecue and magician in the grounds of the school.

Querns Westonbirt is due to open on Monday 9 September 2002, just fifty-six years after Miss Goodworth opened her school on a grey September morning.

Mary Pridgeon

From clinic to school at Paternoster

Paternoster School began life in 1959 as an Occupation Centre of Gloucestershire County Council Health to cater for the needs of up to forty-five 'mentally defectives', as they were called at the time. The supervisor was Miss Winifred Piper and there were thirty-six 'trainees' of all ages on the register. As early as 1965 there were reports of the adults in the centre being 'crowded' in their practical room. In 1967 the first 'Terrapin' building arrived to help with the over-crowding. In 1971, the education of children who were described as 'severely educationally subnormal' became, for the first time, the responsibility of the local education authority. Adults were transferred to an Adult Training Centre in Stroud, and the name of Paternoster School was adopted for the Watermoor Occupation Centre. There were three classes of pupils with trained teachers and assistants while Miss Piper remained as Head Teacher.

At around the same time, an outdoor swimming pool was provided, funded by donations from Cirencester Lions Club. When Miss Piper retired in 1975, Miss Pamela Spiers became the headteacher. She set about changing the ethos of the school from that of a caring institution to an educational one. The Governors, chaired by Mr Cyril Noke, supported her in making demands on the LEA to improve facilities. Numbers in the school increased sufficiently for another teacher to be appointed.

In November 1975 a Parent Teacher Association was formed. The newly formed PTA launched a campaign to buy the first minibus for the school, and, with the help of local people they were successful. The Royal Variety Club Sunshine Coach arrived in 1978. During Miss Spiers' headship the pupils were taken each year on residential visits to the south coast, making use of Girl Guide facilities to which she had access as a District Commissioner for the Guides. She felt that these trips provided an opportunity not only for the pupils, but also a brief respite for their parents. Other new activities introduced were Riding for the Disabled (at the Talland School of Equitation) and Special Olympics. The school adopted the Roman knot as its badge, taken from a mosaic known to be beneath the car park at the front of the school.

Computers began to make their presence felt when some of the pupils travelled to London to receive one as a prize in March 1982. Video cameras were also beginning to be used to record pupils' achievements. Regular events were the annual bonfire party, a summer pool evening, and even trips to Cheltenham for Christmas shopping. Other more exciting trips included a flight in a small aircraft at RAF Brize Norton.

At the end of 1983, Miss Spiers married Mr Ken Come and some of the pupils were taken to the wedding in Purton. Mr Come, a former bank manager, then spearheaded a campaign to buy a new minibus with a tail-lift. Once again local organizations and individuals came up with the goods and the new bus was presented on 18 July 1985. This was Mrs Cottle's farewell to the school as she retired the same day.

In September 1985, Mr Peter Barton became the headteacher. Since that date Paternoster

School, in common with the rest of the educational world, has seen enormous changes, and in 1986 the first Elliott building came into use, followed by another in 1987. The school now had four decent classrooms and a staff room for the first time. The small hall was now available for PE lessons, as half of it was no longer needed for a classroom. An adventure playground was also provided. The Nursery/Assessment unit was becoming well-established as a means of aiding young children to make sufficient progress to enable them to transfer into the local mainstream school. In fact, as demand for places continued to grow, the school was allocated another Elliott building in 1992.

In 1987 the PTA became 'The Friends of Paternoster School', and continued to promote fund-raising events. The school enjoyed a high profile locally and was included, in 1989, on the HTV programme *Highway*, which came from Cirencester, with Sir Harry Secombe singing from the nursery classroom.

The introduction of the National Curriculum required staff to make a detailed appraisal of what and how the pupils were being taught. Initial reluctance to change was not helped when it seemed that pupils with severe learning difficulties were always an afterthought in any national initiatives. However there was a definite broadening of the curriculum. By 1995, the school had acquired yet another Elliott classroom and a hydrotherapy pool on the site of the old swimming pool, funded partly by the LEA and partly by the Friends of the school. A new minibus was also presented to the school by the Lords Taverners in 1995. In 1996 the LEA purchased the clinic from the Health Authority, although work took some time to complete. In 1998 the school took on the form we know today. The buildings first erected as a unit for health services in 1959, were now fully committed to the education of pupils with severe

Sheila Hancock visiting Paternoster School, 2002.

learning difficulties. Occasionally members of the public still turn up, looking for the dentist or chiropodist.

The school has developed specialized facilities in addition to the hydrotherapy pool, such as two sensory rooms, and a sensory garden at the rear. Paternoster School has always aimed to foster links with the local community. Organizations such as Brewery Arts and other bodies have enabled us to develop the creative side of the curriculum. Pupils continue to take part in a wide range of sporting activities through links with local schools, colleges and clubs, including Cirencester Football Academy, and Riding and Sailing for the Disabled. Many pupils individually make links with their local mainstream school.

Now that the LEA is pursuing a policy of inclusion, the next challenge for Paternoster School is to develop its role as a resource centre to support pupils and staff in mainstream schools. This is in addition to providing for those pupils whose needs will continue to be best met within its safe and secure environment.

Vicki Ponsford

6 Wartime Memories

A postcard from Cirencester's first evacuees, 1939.

Strangers and sojourners

Cirencester, as the Roman Corinium, owed its existence to the might of the Roman Army, around whose forts on the Fosse Way the second largest Roman city in Britain developed. Throughout history Cirencester has been connected with military activity, from the cross-border clashes between Saxon and Viking, the destruction of the castle during the Wars of the Roses, the siege of the town by the Royalists in the Civil War and so it goes on. Despite its rather tranquil pace of life and traditional appearance, when there has been trouble in the land Cirencester has been involved.

In more modern times this has been no less apparent. There are still many today who can remember the activity in the town and surrounding area during the Second World War, by the end of which there were at least thirty military establishments within a twelve mile radius of the town. It is hard to imagine that the authorities envisaged this when they designated Cirencester as a safe area for the receipt of evacuees. However throughout the war, evacuees came, sometimes in their hundreds as organized school parties, at other times as family or smaller groups, some officially, others unofficially. Many of the official parties came from the East End of London, from an almost alien city existence, the first arriving two days before the war was declared.

On 31 August 1939 the Cirencester Urban District Council met in special session to hear the Vice Chairman, Mr Tovey, announce that the previously planned Government Evacuation Scheme was to begin the following day. Thus, under the newly appointed Chief Billeting Officer and Town Clerk, Mr Wilkinson, proceedings were set in motion to receive the first consignment of evacuees on that day. Meanwhile in Barking and Dagenham the schools were receiving their orders to put into practise what they had been rehearsing for the past few weeks. Mr Jenks, the headmaster of Bifrons Senior Schools, Barking, was told to be prepared to 'move' at 12.30 p.m. on Friday 1 September, so at the allotted time the children, teachers and helpers assembled at the school with their gas masks and hand luggage and headed for Becontree station from where they journeyed to Paddington to board evacuation train Number 146, which had left the depot at Old Oak Common at 2.15 p.m. At Paddington they were joined by another school from Barking, Cambell Junior and Infants School, with Mr Caswell the headmaster and his staff. Both schools along with a small number of other adults with pre-school children made up a party of over 500 who were destined for Cirencester town,

together with a further 304 children and teachers from other London schools heading for the Cirencester rural district.

The carriages containing all these evacuees were separated from the rest of the train at Kemble and brought into Cirencester town station in the early evening of 1 September. Here the evacuees for the rural district were bussed away to their various destinations while those for the town marched in a procession to the Corn Hall which was arranged as the reception centre. It was recorded at the time that, 'The children made a sorry procession but to give them credit they were surprisingly brave... many of the younger ones clutched teddy bears and dolls as a last link with home.' At the hall a system was activated which had been planned for months by the Urban District Council and The Women's Voluntary Service under their leader Mrs Patience Chestermaster.

By April 1939 the WVS had canvassed the whole town to see who would be able and willing to take in evacuees, as there was no suggestion of compulsion at this stage. Now as the plans were coming to fruition the children

Cirencester looking south from the church tower.

for Stratton were taken to Stratton village hall by coach to meet their foster parents while the rest were taken to their new homes by an army of volunteer assistant billeting officers and their helpers. Many of these children who came on that first train were to stay for the duration and after the initial shock most settled into this strange environment. With the help and co-operation of the local teachers and church workers they soon immersed themselves in school and community life. At the end of September they sent home postcards to tell their families they were all right. Mr Jenks, writing a circular letter to the parents, explained that all was well and that the children were gaining a great deal from their new surroundings. They were using the Baptist and Congregational church halls and had taken up new skills such as book-binding and gardening. Nineteen of them were billeted at the Abbey House in the Abbey grounds which were in the private tenancy of Major Dugdale. They had the run of the grounds and the house and being waited on by servants, were having the time of their lives and all just three minutes from school.

Mr Jenks also wrote to thank the whole community through the local press and this easygoing relationship seems to have developed well with the vast majority of the evacuees who came to the town. There were of course problems and special houses were set up for difficult children and those with bed-wetting problems. Those who took to their new environment also had their problems caused by this new way of life, some of which led to amusing incidents. Evacuees billeted in Gloucester Street came home one evening with minnows from the River Churn, announcing to their hosts that they would be having sardines on toast. Later in the year they came back from the Bowling Green direction bearing arms full of beetroot, lettuce and other vegetables and informed them that they had found them growing wild in a field. The

allotment holder would probably have been less than sympathetic as, in fact, was Mr Caswell when one of his pupils, Harold Robinson, was brought before him.

Harold had been evacuated to Stratton and one day, passing an allotment at the end of Albion Street, seeing the cabbages looking like golf balls on tees, he could not resist the temptation to apply his boot and kicked the heads off all of them. He had never seen cabbages growing before but his unique method of harvesting was frowned upon and when Mr Caswell came up to Stratton School from his base at the Council School in Lewis Lane, Harold – who had been betrayed by someone – was placed before him to receive four whacks of the cane across his stern end. He learned the hard way not to interfere with Digging for Victory!

To occupy any spare time Harold and his friends had, play centres were set up at the Methodist church hall in Ashcroft, The Salvation Army hall in Watermoor Road and the Watermoor Mission Room in Chesterton Lane. The church hall opposite the Malt House in Cricklade Street was also set up to provide a social centre for the evacuees where they could entertain each other, socialise and obtain meals. The latter facility eventually developed into a British Restaurant for the use of the whole community and the evacuees put on shows to entertain themselves and their hosts. There was a wealth of talent amongst them which did much to cheer up the people especially at Christmas time.

The first Christmas of the war was a particularly difficult one and in order to discourage children from going home the Government arranged for special trains to allow parents to visit their children in the reception areas. Cirencester's train came from Paddington on Sunday 10 December and appears to have served its purpose since none of the children seem to have gone home for Christmas. A great effort was made to make it

Evacuees' show at the Church Hall in Cricklade Street.

a memorable Christmas. A large civic party was arranged by a local committee and over a thousand children, evacuees, children of servicemen and the deprived were entertained at the Regal cinema with the film *Alice in Wonderland*, a conjuror and community singing and, of course, refreshments, followed by Bob Fitch the ventriloquist. Father Christmas also made a dramatic visit to Bailey's department store in Cricklade Street after parading around the town in a horse-drawn carriage from the town station. There were so many people in Cricklade Street that he had to throw some of the presents from his sack in front of him to get through the crowd before climbing a ladder on to the shop roof in order to enter his grotto through the fire place. Mr Caswell reported that all his London children had been to see Father Christmas, in fact, over 600 children visited the grotto in the first hour. This must have been rather tiring for Father Christmas who, uncloaked, bore a striking resemblance to Maurice Uzzell, one of the junior employees of Bailey's.

The Christmas party scheme was to be repeated throughout the war and as more and more evacuees came they had to utilise the Gaumont cinema as well as the Regal. Also, as the numbers increased, it was necessary to provide further welfare facilities, so the upper floors of 33 Cricklade Street, owned by John Smith and Sons, seed merchants, were requisitioned for use as an evacuee children's hospital. Daisy Bracher was appointed sister in charge and with her staff was able to provide facilities for twenty-five to thirty-five children suffering from non-infectious diseases plus a daily clinic. Any children with infectious diseases from the town were taken to the Isolation Hospital in Bridge Road. Baunton Mill was converted to an isolation hospital for the children from the rural area. Today the premises of Miss Bracher's former domain look out on the back of the King's Head Hotel and the service road to shops and premises off West Way. When evacuee patients looked out they could view 'a garden, sizeable lawn which provided a veritable sun trap and fruit trees which offered a shady alternative'. It was such a pleasant place that a number of

Stratton evacuees watching a dog fight over Cirencester, 1940.

evacuees have since said that they did all they could to extend their stay in hospital as long as possible. To cater for adult evacuees who were ill, in addition to the Memorial Hospital, provision was made at No. 2 Querns Hill which was requisitioned in September 1940 as an evacuee hostel for adults. With so many evacuee mothers in the town by 1941, to encourage them to take up war work in one of the local ghost factories making weapon components etc, nursery schools were set up at Chesterton Estate and in Abbey Way to cater for their young children and the local pre-school children.

The most tangible evidence for the success of the evacuation scheme in Cirencester seems to have been in the work produced in the schools, and to show what these youngsters could do, exhibitions of their work were put on in various venues in the town. Their skills included the usual crafts along with evidence of practical surveying and architectural appreciation, photographic records and an exceptional creation of a large illustrated needlework map of Cirencester. They also took numerous opportunities to visit local places of interest such as Chedworth Roman Villa and Fairford church. This helped to ease the school accommodation problems for a few hours at least. Other problems that needed attention included the provision of clothing for the evacuees which was not supposed to be the province of the foster families, who received 10s 6d for the first child and 8s 6d for each subsequent child for full board and lodgings. However, with rationing to contend with as well, a clothing depot was set up initially at Querns Lane House for the town's evacuees but later this was moved to the Old Grammar School in Park Lane, then when the rural children were brought into the scheme it moved to the Corn Hall. Here children could obtain secondhand and reconditioned clothing.

Despite all the privations of being away from home and family, most of the evacuees seem to have thrived in their new environment and gained something. Some still today maintain contact with their hosts. Others stayed on after the war or returned later and have continued to contribute to the life of their adopted home. Sad to say, however, there was one evacuee who certainly would have been better off had she stayed at home in her native Eastbourne. Early in January 1941 three-year-old Barbara Andrews was walking along Cricklade Street near the Malt House and holding her mother's hand. A car passed them travelling up the street against the new one way system. This car was followed by a lorry taking a load from Swindon to Manchester. The driver was unaware of the one way system. As the lorry drew alongside Barbara and her mother the wind caught the tarpaulin on the back of the lorry. This struck Mrs Andrews spinning her round so that Barbara was thrown underneath the lorry and killed. There is some irony in this when considering that the one-way system had been put in just a few months earlier by Brigadier Brian Horrocks when he brought his men of the Infantry Brigade to Cirencester immediately after the Dunkirk evacuation. The UDC had been arguing for years about introducing such a scheme.

When drawing up a list of checks and balances it would seem that these strangers to life in a country town gained much from their stay while the townsfolk were given the opportunity to do their bit and at the same time gain a valuable insight into the lives of city dwellers. It is to be hoped that this increased knowledge brought with it a more tolerant attitude. The latter was much needed amongst some of the 'higher class' folk in the

Staff of the Abbey Way Nursery.

May Day at Abbey Way Nursery.

countryside who at first saw evacuees as aliens and let the local press know; some even petitioned parliament to have them sent to poorer parts, such as the valleys of South Wales, where there was more accommodation because large numbers had been relocated and the financial reward for caring for evacuees might be more appreciated amongst those who remained. We even had one local worthy advocating that these strangers be put into camps, a solution much heard of today in relation to others trying to escape from various forms of tyranny. Fortunately from other press reports we know that many of the towns people of Cirencester of all classes held more compassionate views and felt that the best ought to be made of a bad job. These folk fortunately represented the vast majority as did those foster parents who cared for their temporary charges so that the evacuees had a positive experience of life in a market town.

Peter Grace

Refugees in Syde

The village of Syde lies seven miles to the north of Cirencester and one mile to the west of the A417 – the old Roman road called Ermin Street. It was in 1940 a microcosm of rural England. It had a church (part Saxon), a small manor house, a substantial farm house and eight cottages. The people of Syde have always claimed that it is the second smallest parish in the country. No one has ever checked, but that doesn't stop them repeating it with an air of proud certainty.

My family moved there from Lancashire in the spring of 1938, as my father, in partnership with his brother, had taken up the tenancy of Manor Farm and Harcombe Farm. The estate was then owned by the old Squire, Mr Crewdson, who himself came from a Lancashire cotton spinning family. Like many Cotswold villages of the time, Syde had not changed much since the Middle Ages. Everyone who lived in the village worked in the village, either for the squire as estate workers or for my father and uncle on the farm. The population at the time was about thirty-five souls, which is very much the same as it is today. In the Domesday survey of 1086 Syde records eleven inhabitants, so there has hardly been a population explosion in 1,000 years.

My story concerns the Kaskel family who were German refugees during the Second World War. Mr and Mrs Kaskel came as housekeepers to the old squire at the beginning of the war. They had four children who were fostered by Quaker families in different parts of the country so we only met them during the school holidays. They were Ulrich, who was about eighteen, Maria, aged around fourteen and twin boys of ten. They had fled Germany, literally a few days before the war started, because Mrs Kaskel was a member of the congregation of the Confessing Church in Berlin of which Martin Niemoller was the pastor. Pastor Niemoller had opposed Hitler from the very beginning and by 1937 the Nazis could stand it no longer so he was put in Sachsenhausen concentration camp. Mrs Kaskel herself had been taken for interrogation by the Gestapo and it was this which caused them to flee to England.

My family were Methodists and, as well as my father and uncle, their sister also lived in Syde. We held Christian meetings in our houses every Thursday night and Mrs Kaskel often came to preach. As well as being fluent in English, she also spoke French and regularly helped my brother with his French homework. When the war ended in Europe the village held a fete to celebrate VE day. It was unanimously agreed that Mr and Mrs Kaskel should be the guests of honour and that Mrs Kaskel should judge all the competitions,

Refugees in Syde.

so much were they loved and regarded by the people of the village.

Whether we are the second smallest parish in the country I cannot be certain but I could be almost sure that we were the only village that celebrated VE Day with a German family as the special guests.

The Methodists in Syde for many years held an annual Christian rally in our barn. In 1959 my mother wrote to Mrs Kaskel, now living in Frankfurt, and asked her if there would be any chance of Martin Niemoller coming to Syde to speak at our meeting. How she managed it I don't know, but that summer, Martin Niemoller, who at that time was one of the most famous churchmen in the world, came to preach at the rally before approximately 600 people. He stayed overnight with my uncle but came to our house for tea and I've always said that for us it was like entertaining St Paul. He told us of his experiences in the concentration camps – but only because we pressed him to. The horrors he described were unspeakable. In the Great War he had been a U-boat commander and he was something of a hero to the German people so the Nazis dare not let him die.

In 1995 Syde held another celebration, this time to commemorate fifty years of peace since the end of the Second World War. Everybody who was in Syde village in 1945 came back. I managed to trace Graham, one of the Kaskel twins who was living in Somerset and, like his parents half a century earlier, he and his family were welcomed with great affection by all those who remembered him. He said to me, 'You people in Syde never realised how safe you made us feel during those dark days when we were refugees'.

This story is a testimony of how the love of ordinary people transcends all barriers, even as the separate nations to which they belong tear each other apart.

Malcolm Whitaker

Memories of war and farming

During the Second World War everyone was called upon to do war duties in addition to their daily tasks and on the farm here we formed a platoon of the LDV as soon as volunteers were asked for in the bad days of 1940, the farm manager taking the post of Commander. Those like myself who had stock to look after had very few leisure hours to spend and on several occasions I had no sleep for as long as forty-eight hours. Having two parades and one guard duty to do each week kept us fully occupied, and knowing the district well was of course a great advantage to us when out on training. The difficulties came when doing a night patrol on unaccustomed land. It was only too easy to fall in a ditch or trip over the electric fencing or get one's clothes caught on a barbed wire, and once several of us nearly fell into a quarry.

My special knowledge stood me in good stead during our manoeuvres, for our platoon had orders to attack the headquarters which were situated in the old Militia Barracks close by the Cecily Hill Park Gates. Two of us were detailed off to make an attempt to get inside without being seen and although I lost my 'second' in the darkness and despite the fact that the barracks were well-guarded I managed to get inside and take the staff prisoner. How I did it I never told anyone but kept the secret to myself. Headquarters' staff said that I used a secret tunnel, but in fact I crept up to one of the houses in the drive below the barracks (they are of the villa type, all in a row), knocked quietly on the door, and asked the maid to let me through into the garden at the back. Once there I climbed on a fowl pen and scaled the wall, not without making considerable noise which, however, nobody seemed to notice. From there it was comparatively easy to sneak into the canteen and catch all the officers there for they weren't expecting an attack from the town-side of the

Cirencester Home Guard, June 1943.

building and they were all sitting around knowing that the other sides were well patrolled!

I spent some very interesting times and some very sad ones during the time I was a member of the Home Guard but on the whole I never regretted giving this service for the love of my country, not in the First World War – I was too young to be called up – and in the last one too old. The worst moments came when I was out on patrol, the German planes roaring overhead with the sky all to themselves and nothing to challenge them. Then the bombs would drop and sad thoughts would come to me.

Though I would like to see some more oxen at work on the farm I do not think I should like to return to the old working conditions, for life is much easier than it used to be. Two simple things that are laid on today

are water and electricity, and although the latter has only just reached my own house it is certainly a blessing. It is remarkable the great improvement that has taken place in the lighting up of the farm for way back in the early days of the century the only source of light that we had was the old tallow candles. These were usually joined together by the wicks in bunches of half a dozen when bought, and the light from them was no more than a glimmer so that one was unable to distinguish the colour of a horse in the stables. Later on they were improved by the 'short twelve' candle, usually carried about in the old-fashioned horn lantern with six sides and I have often used them myself. When the hurricane lamp was introduced it was a real step forward and now there are a variety of pressure lamps of the mantle type which give a light similar to gas.

Working around the farm in the dark can be very dangerous and once when going into a pitch black house I tripped over a steel-fined rake with the result that one of the points entered my knee and laid me up for a fortnight. Another of our men fell over a block of wood at night and twisted his knee so badly that he was kept away from work for nearly twelve months. One dark morning I entered the hay shed and it was there that I got the biggest fright of my life for, bending down to gather an armful of fodder, I put my arm round an old sow who had snuggled up in the hay for warmth. I don't know who was the most frightened, me or the sow, but it was my usual practice to pick the hay up with a fork and had I done so that morning I must surely have done serious damage to the beast!

It is a wonder that more fires were not caused by the old fashioned way of lighting for there was always a lot of combustible material lying about the barns and yards and some of the farm hands were careless in the extreme, putting down their lanterns at anytime and anywhere without a thought as to what might happen. With electricity available nearly everywhere I feel that all farms should be kept well lit-up at least during the winter months, not only for convenience but for the safety of all concerned. With all the progress made in improving the working conditions and with the changing times some of the pleasant things that made life seem more worth while living have gradually been forgotten, and owing to two world wars the young farmers of today never knew of the old customs which brought master and man closer together.

I myself have been fortunate in working for a family which has always had the interests of its workers at heart, and many country folk regret the passing of the old squires who usually saw to it that their workers were well-provided for, it being the smaller farmers without much capital behind them who under-paid their men and worked them like slaves simply because they could not afford to do otherwise.

One thing that I miss particularly and which I think might well be revived is the old Harvest Home, today remembered only by the churches. In my youth this was a grand evening, usually held in 'Ye Olde Wagon Shed', with plenty of beer and cider to drink (and home-brewed at that) and this caused everyone to be really bright and merry so that the singing and devilment was carried on till midnight. I can also remember that when we were working in the hay and harvest fields the men would stop work every two hours to have their tots of ale, which put them in a real good spirit for the job and I can testify that in the old days twice as much work was done between morning and night as is done at the present time.

Another annual event was the Rook Shoot at which all the local farmers and farm-hands who had guns (and a mixed collection they were) would get together to shoot as many rooks as they could. We boys would collect the rooks as they fell (some of them would go into the cottagers' rook pies afterwards) and when the guns stopped for refreshments they would assemble us together and conduct a sports meeting with races and jumping and such like and everyone would go home thoroughly satisfied.

Yes, times have changed, and a few years ago it was brought home to me when we had some school children to help us pick the potatoes up. When they arrived some of them were grown-up young chaps of fifteen, as big as I am, but what really amused me was when they got their pints of milk out and began to drink them. When I was their age I used to have a half bottle of water and filled it up with tea straight out of the pot with no milk or sugar in it, and that had to do for whole day.

In the old days boys were not so much mollycoddled and I remember being set to root hoeing when I was not much older than some of the young gentlemen who came potato picking, and how it made me ache for it took two or three days to get one's back set. Usually this was done as piecework, that is to say one was paid so much an acre, and not so long ago I heard a very good story about this job, and a true one. A farmer went up to one of his men who was turnip hoeing to see how he was getting on. As he stood there looking on, the old fellow began to act a bit awkward, not liking the farmer's presence of course, and started to cut them all up. This was too much for the farmer and he cried out 'Careful, Gaarge, you be cutting 'em all up,' to which Gaarge replied 'Ay, an' if thee stops yer much longer, Gaffer, I'll cut whole field up!'

Edward Charles Smith

War work in Cirencester

I was born in 1922, Mother a domestic cook and Father a chauffeur, in one of a row of seventeen Cotswold stone cottages off a street in the centre of Cirencester. A pump stood in the middle of the road for a water supply and the men washed there, stripped to the waist, on coming home from work. Some of these worked at Cole and Lewis bacon factory. I can still recall the sound of their iron-tipped clogs coming along the brick path at the back of the cottages. There was a lavatory for every two to three houses. Our bread was delivered by hand truck, the milk by horse and cart and all our vegetables were grown either at the allotment in Love Lane or the garden outside the house. Our meat come from the Cricklade Street butcher who we called Bacon Burge and who fattened his own beasts, butchered and sold them (no additives or allergies then). The cattle market was on Mondays and we had to be sure, when later we moved to Siddington Road, to close the gate on that day because sheep and cattle were brought into town on the hoof with drovers at front and back.

Watermoor in the early '30s had a general and sweet shop, run by Molly Davenport, a post office and grocery run by Mr and Mrs Cave and daughter Dinah, a baker's, 'Doughy Andrews', Mr Barber's grocery with a strange machine which produced fizzy drinks, and a butcher's shop run by Alan Arthurs. Monty Caudle was the taxi proprietor, Lumber Lou sold second-hand goods and Mr Humphreys sold stuff from his smallholding alongside the canal. There was Baldwin's builders and Charlie Baker the undertaker.

The GWR railway ran a train from Watermoor to Swindon around 7 o'clock in the morning. Many local tradesmen, wheelwrights, engineers, blacksmiths, etc. travelled to and from the Great Western Railway works and you could set your clock by the 7.00 a.m. (or was it 7.30 a.m.?) train. From Watermoor long trains of coal wagons came through regularly, each truck bearing the name of a Welsh colliery, we'd watch them going over Watermoor bridge.

Our childhood games were led by the seasons. When evenings were dark the older boys had a hiding game – some of them hid in alleyways with hand torches, in dark corners, up trees and when the searchers spotted them they called 'Jack Jack shine your light' and they were then found. Only boys played this game and only boys played 'John John Jonnie-oh' where a line of boys would line up, bent backs crouched over behind the first one, head against a door or fence while the others would run and leap as far as possible over the bent backs. When evenings were lighter and dry, the girls would be skipping with ropes or playing hopscotch and the boys would play marbles or whip tops up and down the street. Nobody in our street had a car – only the lucky ones had a bike, so we could safely play street games, 'Sheep, sheep come home', 'Granny's footsteps' or Tag, all involving catching and chasing. Winter times in bad weather, when we couldn't get outside, we devoted ourselves to comics, *Chicks* and *Tiger Tim* and for the boys *Wizard* and *Hotspur* and amongst ourselves there was a good swapping system.

Summer days we spent in groups of four or five brothers, sisters and friends and would go to Cirencester Park with a picnic – usually eaten at once on arrival at the Octagon. We were watched over by Mr Bradley who wore an olive green uniform with brass buttons and olive green bowler. If he thought we might be up to mischief – trying to climb trees or anything – he'd blow his whistle and we would be off. Much of this was unchanged until 1938/9 when I had left school and gone to work for the council as Clerk to the ARP committee. The council members at this time were about a dozen or so, retired military men, ex-headmasters, local builders etc, non-political and representing the whole of the town. The Warden, Demolition, Decontamination, Rescue, Fire Services were being set up and arrangements were being made for evacuees to come to Cirencester which had been designated a Reception Area. Things were very busy on Sunday 3 September 1939 and we were all at work and the Clerk and Assistant Clerk broke off to listen to the radio and hear Mr Chamberlain announce the declaration of war. It was noon on a warm sunny Sunday and they walked back into the boardroom and told me, one after the other, 'It's war' and I'll never forget that moment.

Our evacuees came from the docklands areas, Barking, Dagenham etc, some accompanied by parents and some on their own and of course some teachers, too. In time they settled down, problems got sorted out, many stayed and some went home. The council became involved in providing furniture as well as accommodation and I remember people from London who had been bombed out arriving at the council office with coats over their nightclothes wanting help. The British Restaurant in Cricklade Street was organised by the council and opened in the early years of the war to provide cooked breakfasts and lunches for war workers and others. There were paid staff of course but also many volunteers involved in keeping this important facility going as in many other aspects of war provision.

Part of my job was getting involved in issuing gas masks which we were required to

Cirencester Urban District Council officials, 1939-1944.

carry at all times in their cardboard containers, civilian gas masks for non-services. General Service gas masks for the local ARP combined services and large 'Mickey Mouse' gas masks for small children under a year – toddlers had a red-coloured one with a rubber snout sort of valve which made a noise like blowing a raspberry. Lots of other things happened like the setting up of 'Buffer Food Depots' at secret locations, instructions concerning these came from Whitehall and had a secret code name. An air raid control centre was established in cellar spaces beneath the Board Room in the council offices. It was made gas proof with thick double doors. Desks with telephones direct to Fire, Police, Warden and the other services were manned twenty-four hours, day or night and I was responsible for the watch of volunteers. I must say that this was never a problem, from local people and from folks whose business or other reasons brought them to Cirencester there were always offers to man the phone. Several London firms relocated to Cirencester and eventually some established themselves here. With them came smart young people who soon integrated into everything, joined in tennis and other clubs, married and stayed here and made a special contribution to social life such as it was in wartime.

Fund-raising became important, we had War Weapons Week, Spitfire Week – special events were the Police Ball, Young Farmers Ball, Red Cross Ball, and the special floor at the Bingham Hall would be laid, or else we danced in the Corn Hall, or the church hall, or nearby village halls. It was possible to go dancing somewhere every night. The American army staffed the US hospital in Cirencester Park, many young airmen were learning to fly at No. 3 FTS, South Cerney. After Dunkirk, trainloads of soldiers came through Watermoor station so there were lots of dancing partners.

Before the war started we began to be aware of refugees from Nazi Germany coming to town and as time went on their extended families came too; the young men joined the Auxiliary Military Pioneer Corps (AMPs) and the wives joined various voluntary services, we called them AMP wives.

On the Gloucester road just outside Cirencester a large group of typical wartime huts appeared and eventually housed 'Displaced Persons' – driven from their homes by Nazi persecution - they were mostly Poles and we became aware of their occupation of these bare barrack-like buildings. Gradually curtains appeared at windows, mats were shaken and hung outside on fences and in time the occupants in their various ways joined in wartime life in Cirencester. Young girls got jobs in town, in spite of language difficulties, young men joined the services, some returned to their native land and some settled here. What was noticeable throughout the entire war were the great number of young servicemen from various countries and their different uniforms. Our own soldiers, sailors and airmen were familiar, the Americans with their good quality cloth and tailoring, US nurses from the hospital up in the park, beautifully dressed and smartly turned out with lovely brown leather shoes and warm woollen beige cardigans. Australians, South Africans, Canadians, many European countries and a handsome Norwegian pilot in a uniform of grey; he married a local girl and they are still happily married in Norway.

So many changes, from a quiet Cotswold market town of seven thousand inhabitants to a bustling and busy place of many light industries whose population more that doubled, clinging to its Roman past but not changed all that much. Two useful schemes were organized by the clerk to the council: one was the pig club: members paid a fee on joining and pigs were purchased from Brockworth, near Gloucester, kept near Cirencester and fed and at killing time the fresh meat was shared.

Initially lots were drawn to determine who had a ham after curing and if successful it meant that at the next killing you would get a hock.

Not everyone had an allotment or a garden, even though provision was made for 'Digging for Victory'. Land was made available on a farm at Cranhams Lane, Chesterton and the farmer drew out numbered furrows across the field and stored manure in the bottom. Members turned up with their seed potatoes, planted and covered them in and in due time, in late August and September it was time to dig them up. I remember helping my father to fill hessian sacks and getting them home somehow on a bicycle.

Mrs M. Baynham

A land girl's story

I was born in a tiny cottage in South Cerney and moved to Cirencester in 1926. We had a new house at the Victoria Road end of Purley Avenue, next to the garage on the corner, which my father managed and to which he had cycled daily from South Cerney. Growing up in Cirencester was idyllic; no hustle and bustle, no rat race. That came much later. We knew all our neighbours as Mr and Mrs whoever, so there was no familiarity and use of christian names, nor was there in schools, hospitals and places of work. We were taught a healthy respect for law and order and we were taught, at home, to be mindful of others and their property. Windows and doors could be safely left open, and we had freedom of movement on foot and as we grew older, on bicycles. There was no fear of molestation, mugging or vandalism. If a neighbour was ill, someone was always ready to mind children, shop or provide some nourishing soup. In the town, shops very rarely changed hands, and the name you saw on the door was the person or a member of the family you saw and who

dealt with you. The population figure was 7,000. I started at the council school in Lewis Lane aged five years, the Infants being the only time I was 'Co-ed'. I moved in to the Girls School aged seven years and to the Grammar School at eleven. Life was very different there. From the time we started in form 11A (2a) we were told our aim was the School Certificate (Cambridge) to be taken in Form V Teachers wore gowns, and caps on special occasions. Each taught their own subject and came to us in our classroom, apart from Art, Physics and Chemistry when we went to the studio or laboratory. They were in the Boys School – a weird experience. Girls and boys did not fraternise and if two pupils in uniform and of different sex were seen walking together by staff or prefects, detention was the form of punishment, even if you were brother and sister, similarly if you were seen in uniform eating ice cream or fish and chips.

Uniform had to be strictly adhered to: navy gym slips, white blouses, navy knickers, black stockings, black lace-up outdoor shoes, black with a bar. Luckily, the year I started it had been decided white ankle socks might be better with the light blue summer dresses. Navy dresses and the dreaded black stockings had been worn before. We played hockey and netball in winter. Girls did not go to the gym as it was not considered lady-like. Summer brought tennis or a weekly visit to the open-air swimming pool, a season ticket for which enabled a daily visit to the baths during May to September (not Sundays) costing 3s 6d (Sundays cost more).

School meals had not started then so those who came on the school bus had to bring sandwiches for lunch.

On the death of King George V, those of us who lived nearby were sent home to get a black armband, go back to school then go in a crocodile to the Market Place for the proclamation of Edward VIII. I wonder how many mothers would be at home and able to provide a blackarm band these days?. Schooldays continued a carefree and happy time. Out of school activities included Abbey Brownies and Abbey Guides. We met in a hut in the Abbey grounds – at that time the property of a local family. The daughter was a Guide Commissioner. The Girls Friendly Society met in the town hall above the church porch. Then came the threat of war, and what changes that brought about! The blackout, evacuees, rationing, clothing coupons, petrol coupons, identity cards, gas masks, and after war was declared in September 1939, fear of air raids, bombs and lives lost. Four of father's petrol pumps were taken over by the War Department leaving one for his use. Different members of the forces came to fill army vehicles: New Zealanders stationed at Siddington Hall and working as foresters, Gloucestershire Regiment, Pioneer Corps, Engineers, etc., and on one occasion at 11p.m. a contingent of Americans. The noise that time was incredible – men and vehicles everywhere.

When the new term started, some of the boys' classrooms had been taken over by the army, so there was a lot of sorting out to be done, and at the end there was no room for Form V girls, of which I was one. We were directed to the Masonic Hall in the Avenue. All we had to work with was in our satchels. I had pens, pencils, crayons – no felt-tips or biros in those days, French vocabulary notebook, the *Epic of Mount Everest* holiday reading in readiness for the exam, and a note book. We spent the day playing word games. Things were gradually sorted out, the army left and we were able to get back to school and get to work. While taking the School Certificate I was offered a job, a fourth girl was needed to take the place of a young male employee called up for service in the Royal Navy, and a friend who worked at the office thought I would be leaving school in the July. I had always assumed that if I passed the

School Cert' I would stay another two years and study for Higher School Cert' and if I managed to pass that, maybe university and probably a career in teaching. The war changed so many lives and plans. I was accepted for the job and started at the end of July. We four girls had all taken the place of men who had been called up and it was assumed we would remain there for the duration. The War Department had other ideas. Twice a letter was sent to the office saying we would have to do War Work, each time the Chief Secretary (boss of the Office) was told we could stay, but the third letter received in April '42 advised that if we had not found work in either of the under mentioned, we would be directed: Nursing, NAAFI, Royal Observer Corps, Post Office Telephones and Maintenance, munitions factory, Womens Land Army. I chose the last, filled in a form, had an interview and a medical, and was gone by the end of April.

Four weeks training at Fieldgrove Farm Bitton, between Bath and Bristol. Ten shillings per week all found, next four weeks employed by the Gloucestershire War Agricultural Executive Committee (were we trained by them? – absolutely not), money went up to £2 something, board and lodging taken out, and an initial uniform was provided by the WLA but replacements had to be bought. At Fieldgrove we lived in the Farm House, there were three permanent girls and sixteen of us, two new ones arrived on a Monday and two moved out. The farmer lived in the farm cottage with his mother and our WLA forewoman lodged with them. We had a housekeeper to rule us. She often did not agree with things the farmer wanted so that caused a bit of interest, but on the whole it was not too bad.

The resident girls took it in turns to call us in the morning some time before 6 a.m. We went to the kitchen for a cup of tea, two slices of bread with the butter allocation for the day

Old Gloucester breed cattle on the Bathurst Estate.

and a half pot of jam which had to last the week. One morning during my stay we had margarine – not butter – no one was at all pleased. We were not putting up with that, we were entitled to our butter, and we got it!

One of the resident girls on my first morning gave me a bucket and stool, showed me a cow and said 'get on with it' no instruction, no showing, and when I asked 'How?' she said 'Squeeze and pull, you'll get some milk eventually'. Ha ha! Squeeze pull squeeze pull – nothing – hours later, or so it seemed, back came my tormentor, sat down and effortlessly soon had the bucket almost half full of foaming milk. It took me about a week to really get going, by which time my hand and arms had permanent 'pins and needles', but I was promoted to one of the milking sheds instead of just one cow and a very raw recruit in a small shed. Then for two weeks I had to machine-milk, which I did not like at all. Milking of course was twice daily. In between we hoed and singled kale and mangolds, cleaned out loose boxes and tidied the granary. One day, two of us went with the tractor driver to plant potatoes on another farm. Calves of all sizes had to be roped and taken for a walk to the end of the farm road and back.

One morning the farmer who was always out waiting for us to appear, told me to take one of the other girls and harness one of the two horses to a float and go off to one of the fields for a load of vetch. Well, that was different – biggest problem was catching the horse – they were both of the opinion that we were there to play. A fortnight before I was due to leave

Fieldgrove the farmer told me he was sending me to Dursley where I would be with eleven other girls all trained by him and it was machine-milking, very modern, just the thing, not for me though I wanted a small farm, hand-milking, but it appeared I had very little choice. The following Monday though I was told to go and see someone at the hostel. This was to see one of the ladies who interviewed me and who knew another girl was needed in Cirencester Park. Would I like to go? Would I? A herd of Gloucester cows, forty to milk twice daily and all other duties connected to dairy farming; it sounded wonderful. I duly left Fieldgrove on the Friday evening, having saved up my half-days a week off during the second month I was there in order to take a weekend at home, and met the farm bailiff on the Monday morning. He took me to the Mansion House where I was to stay and to meet the housekeeper. It soon became apparent that this was not going to work. The lady had fixed mealtimes and was unable to be flexible to cope with the vagaries of cows so I suggested it might be better if I lived at home, this was agreed.

I cycled to the sheds in the Park. We started at 6 a.m., when the stove had to be lit for the cooling system and the cows fetched from the field. The smallest cow in the herd, Yum Yum by name, was usually at the gate and mooed, whether as a welcome to us or to tell the other cows to come, we knew not. On rare occasions usually if it was foggy she would be missing and I went to look for her calling her name, no response until I almost reached her – when she would moo as much as to say 'you took your time' and wait for a stroke and a few words before we could join the others. Once in the yard the cows made their own ways to the stalls, heavy milkers first. Just one cow had to be difficult – Araminta –

small milk yield but determined to be first in, she was soon sorted out but not by us, but by the rightful first comers. We had to award her top marks for trying, and then eventually going out to wait her turn.

There were two cowmen and we three girls. On the two days a week when we were all there we each milked eight cows, on the other five days one or other of us had the day off so we had to milk ten each. Milking finished about 8.30 a.m. so home for breakfast then back to clean the shed and – depending on the season – perhaps to top and tail mangolds or climb the silage tower and get the silage out for feed, the first was done in a shed, nice, the second hard work and smelly. We discovered the silage had to be fed out in the yard as in the mangers it tainted the milk and as it was a Tuberculosis attested herd that would never do. If we had a slack period we could always go wooding to stoke the fire. One frosty morning we had a message that someone had left a gate open and four calves had escaped. We found them in a kale field; it took us ages to round them up and we were soaking wet going up and down the rows.

There were two American hospitals in the Park and some afternoons, coming back from lunch, the boys would be out in the sun in their blue pyjamas and maroon dressing gowns. Suddenly a dust cloud appeared in the distance and they all made for the trees on either side – a jeep containing Military Police was the cause of the dust and the hasty retreat.

We often had a visit from the hounds. Hunting season over, they had to be exercised and where better than in the Park? Their kennels were near the Tetbury Road entrance. During the war we had double summer time to enable haymaking and harvest to continue until 10 or 11 p.m. This meant we could only gradually change the milking schedule by a few minutes daily; it was no good expecting the cows to appreciate the extra hour.

Christmas morning was magical. We knew it would not be fair to take time off so we were all working, and at some point the cowman said, 'Come outside and take a look'. There had been a sharp frost, the moon was shining, trees, grass and spiders webs looked like tinsel and the stars were shining; truly beautiful.

One of the girls decided she had enough of the Land Army and went back to Lancashire. She was not replaced, as soon afterwards machines were installed and hand-milking was out – unfortunately. Some months later the other girl went home to Bristol and was replaced by a girl I trained with, her home was in Sheffield. The war was coming to an end and there was talk of Peace. On the day the WLA release dates were given, my office boss came to see when I could go back to them. My little bit for the War Effort was over and my WLA overcoat returned as requested.

Hilda Crawford

7 Shops, Pubs and Hostelries

Gegg the grocer

In her book *Little Eden*, Eva Figes stated that she happened to be passing near Cirencester some years ago on her way from London to another part of the Cotswolds, and suddenly began to recognize certain lanes, fields, trees and houses. She then remembered being a wartime evacuee, and living in Cirencester for a short time, some thirty years previously. She vowed to return, and, on doing so, found herself transported 'back in the past', in a 'landscape unchanged and frozen in time, into a sanctuary of the past.'

Many who were born in Cirencester, and moved elsewhere in later life, have returned to this area in retirement. In my own case, I attended Chesterville School, Lewis Lane School and then went on to Cirencester Grammar School, before leaving the town for university, and living away for fifty years. I have now retired to Cirencester, thanks to the good nature of my wife, and am experiencing this 'sanctuary of the past' phenomenon. There are some physical changes in and around Cirencester, such as new buildings, roads and even dual-carriageways, but we can still walk along old streets, pass familiar buildings, walk in the Park, visit surrounding villages, and enjoy the Cotswold landscape.

It is, of course, possible to go farther 'back in the past', and try to learn a little more about, perhaps, some immediate past members of our family whom we have never known or had the pleasure of meeting. This is facilitated by living in the area they occupied, and having easier access to living relatives, with their family stories, access to local Record Offices, Parish Registers, churchyards and other archives. I have heard stories, and found memorabilia, of my great-grandfather, who had a grocery business in the town 100-150 years ago, and was therefore eager to have the opportunity of finding out more about Joseph Gegg, a nineteenth-century Cirencester grocer.

Joseph was born in Withington in 1833, the fourth son of Joseph Gegg the local boot and shoemaker. In his private life, Joseph senior was involved in the foundation and running of the Wesleyan Methodist chapel in the village, which was registered for religious worship by Protestant Dissenters in 1854. Joseph junior left home before the age of eighteen (1851 census) and seems to have been given a grocery apprenticeship in Maidstone, Kent. By 1858 he had returned to Cirencester determined to set up as a master grocer, and was married in August of that year to Jane Collett, the daughter of Henry Collett, a shoemaker, of Chedworth. The same month, aged twenty-five, he was received into membership of the Cirencester Congregational church, Sheep Street, on transfer from Week Street chapel, Maidstone.

Having completed his apprenticeship, married, and returned to Cirencester, he took over a grocery business, situated at Nos 183-184 Gloucester Street, on 2 August 1858. The property consisted of a large shop with staff accommodation above, and also an adjacent

Joseph Gegg and his wife Jane, c. 1850.

house for his residential use. It was situated near Powell's School, between Sheppard's Place and The Loyal Volunteer Inn. The latter is now a private house, but was the old Gloucester Street Theatre from 1799 until 1820.

The old photograph below illustrates the appearance of Gloucester Street around 1910, with horses and carts, cycles, ladies with long black dresses, and Messrs Gegg & Son, Family Grocers on the extreme-left of the picture. Outside the shop would have been one of the horse and traps for delivering grocery to surrounding villages. This modern picture shows the scene in Gloucester Street with an absence of busy commercial activity now replaced by passive car parking. The population of Cirencester was around 6,000 at the time Joseph commenced. It rose to 6,336 in 1861 and it is interesting to find no fewer that seven grocery shops in Gloucester Street in this year, according to contemporary commercial

View of Gloucester Street, c. 1910.

Nos 23 and 24 Gloucester Street today.

directories. Competition must have been fierce, although there were many residential properties in this important road leading out of Cirencester. There were also numerous alleys and side streets.

By 1872, Joseph and Jane had a family consisting of a daughter Kate, and two sons, Joseph and Frank. A second daughter died of a throat infection with consequent swelling, at the age of three, and was buried in the Dissenters' Burial Ground in Watermoor Road. There were no antibiotics available in the nineteenth century.

Joseph created a very successful business, employing several assistants, and usually having at least one grocer's apprentice. He remained in business for fifty-eight years, retiring in 1912. A 1905 picture shows Joseph and Jane photographed by their son Fred Gegg who had photographic studios at Stow-on-the-Wold and

Evesham. Joseph Gegg appears on the 1897 photograph of all members of the Cirencester Tradesmen's Society, as well as his two sons Joseph and Frank. A great assortment of general groceries and Italian goods were sold at the Gloucester Street shop. For example, six varieties of tea: Assam, Choice Black China, Darjeeling, Indian and Ceylon, Orange Pekoe, and an interesting tea named Young Hyson Gunpowder. Schweitzer's Cocoatina, Van Houten's Cocoa and Best Trinidad Cocoa Nibs were available in the cocoa section, together with some fourteen varieties of spices. There were fifty-three types of biscuits, including Bath Olivers, Garibaldi, Palermo, Queen and Extra Toast, as well as the usual varieties. It is interesting to note eleven different types of candles, including cowslip wax, snuffles dips, red sperms, etc, and fifteen soaps, including Hudson's Dry, Best London Mottled, and

Joseph and Jane Gegg and their children, c. 1872.

Vinolia. Brooms, brushes and mats of all descriptions could be bought, and house flannels, wax matches, tapers, black lead, powder blue, Coleman's starch, borax, and brass polish. Messrs Gegg & Son advertised many of these items in local newspapers, booklets, and the *Dyer Street Monthly* – a Journal of Congregationalism in Cirencester.

Some memorabilia of the business still exists, although ninety years have elapsed since its closure. I have one original copy of a grocery book as issued to all customers for their weekly grocery list, and have been fortunate to find six stone jars engraved with Gegg & Son, Family Grocer, Cirencester. The latter were used to sell vinegar and other solutions and were loaned to customers. Patent medicines and pills were also available at local grocers. Elixirs were elegantly packaged, with extravagant claims. Pills could be obtained for both head and stomach pains, in fact, treating any organ, and usually

contained a combination of soap and a mild laxative.

As with all businesses, certain problems arose from time to time. In the 1860s a report in the *Wilts and Gloucestershire Standard* drew attention to a court case: James Munday v Joseph Gegg. This was an action to recover damages of five pounds for assault. The plaintiff was a journeyman tripe-seller, aged sixty, living in Cirencester and the defendant Joseph Gegg, grocer carrying on business in the town. In the summer of 1858 the plaintiff, with a partner, ran up an account amounting to about two pounds, and Joseph had difficulty in claiming payment. Munday later made an appearance in the shop and, in a drunken state, grossly insulted Joseph's wife, Jane. The following morning he again entered the shop drunk and behaved in a disgraceful manner. Refusing to leave, and brandishing his fists, Joseph pushed him out of the shop. Unfortunately the doorstep was somewhat slippery from frosty weather and the plaintiff pitched across the road, apparently receiving severe bruising and cutting his head. The judge gave a judgment, remarking that the conduct of the plaintiff was very bad, but that the defendant was not justified in acting as he had done. Damages of four guineas for the plaintiff resulted.

Joseph was a member and deacon of the Congregational church in Dyer Street and at a subsequent church meeting he stated that the man by whom he had been recently sued in the county court had been to him and acknowledged that he had sworn falsely against him. This confession the wretched man had made, with tears, to Mr Gegg in his shop. In the church minutes of the meeting, Psalm 37 was quoted, which states: 'The Lord saves righteous men and protects them in

Joseph Gegg and his wife Jane, c. 1905.

Advertisements from a local pamphlet.

times of trouble. He helps them and rescues them. He saves them from the wicked because they go to Him for protection'.

Joseph kept a diary, and his entry for 2 August 1878 stated that it was twenty years ago on that day that 'I took to the shop and stock in Gloucester Street. I am very thankful for all past mercies and hopeful for the future. Not unto us be the Glory, but unto Him be all praise, who has blessed us causing His face to shine upon us'.

Joseph carried on his business until 1912. He had three sons, one of whom later assisted and continued the business until his ill health caused closure of Messrs Gegg & Son. Another son, Frank, had a coal merchant's business at the Canal Wharf until 1921, and the third son, Fred, became a professional photographer and moved to Evesham. Joseph's wife Jane died in 1898, and he remarried in 1902, at the age of sixty-nine, Jane Reeve, who was aged thirty-nine and the daughter of

James Reeve of Bowling Green Farm, Cirencester.

Joseph's obituary in the *Wilts & Glos Standard* recorded a summary of his life: 'The death occurred on 11 August 1922 at his residence in Watermoor Road, Cirencester, of Mr Joseph Gegg, one of the oldest townsmen, he having reached his ninetieth year. Mr Gegg, who has for sometime been living in retirement, for many years carried on an extensive grocery business in Gloucester Street, first alone and afterwards in partnership with his eldest son. He had a wide country connection in Chedworth, Withington, and the surrounding Cotswold district. An earnest Free Churchman, being a member of the Congregational body and a convinced Liberal in politics, Mr Gegg was also a prominent member of the old Cirencester Temperance Society, and, in earlier life, took an active interest in the movements which those associations connect. He was held in sincere regard by his friends and neighbours. Mr Gegg was an active deacon in the Congregational church, and, when declining health compelled him to relinquish this office, his valued services in this capacity were recognized by conferring upon him the dignity of honorary deacon'.

In concluding this story I now know much more about the life, times and trials of Joseph Gegg, (1833-1922), Master Grocer, my immediate ancestor, and a prominent tradesman in Cirencester in the nineteenth century. Transportation 'back into the past' has been an interesting and rewarding experience, and an insight into the times before supermarkets.

Brian Gegg

Original stone jars from Messrs Gegg and Son.

The Fleece Hotel, Market Place, Cirencester.

Inns of Cirencester

The Fleece

The records of the Bull Club state: 'first known date 1750, Joseph Pitt owner, in occupation of Thomas Leddiard. 1753. John Saunders at The Fleece. 1765 Wm Brewer, Innholder, Fleece. Charles Hiever (sic) surrenders lease to Mary Saunders, Fleece Inn in Dyer Street, otherwise Chipping Street on 20 June 1777. Samuel Rudder printer and bookseller had premises on the east side. The Fleece is also mentioned, by name only, in 1759 and 1794. By 1830 The Fleece was known as a Commercial Hotel and it has been described as a hotel ever since. Street names seem to chop and change, for in 1840 James Trinder gave his address as being in the Market Place. A Sale notice issued during the Trinder (father and later his son) time at the Fleece mentioned a triangular piece of ground now used as a quoits and skittles pitch, in the occupation of Mr James Trinder as a yearly tenant.

The Fleece does not seem to have been tied to any particular brewery, though Earl Bathurst was the owner of the property. In 1876 The Fleece was advertised as a Commercial Hotel & Posting House. The omnibus, mentioned in an advertisement, left from outside The Fleece daily at 4.15 p.m. for Fairford.

James Trinder junior was local agent for Messrs Worthington & Co., Burton on Trent Ales, an early mention of a brewery with much larger than local coverage. The rateable list for 1903 shows The Fleece as second-only to The Kings Head in importance. An advertisement by L.T. Campion proprietor in 1915 mentions stabling, posting parties catered for, and free garage also billiards. A bus meets all trains, probably a horse-drawn one. By 1927 the hotel was under the control of County Hotels Ltd and was run by a series of managers. Later it became part of the Trust House Forte Group. The Fleece continues as a well patronised hotel, having recently acquired the adjacent premises, previously The Sun Inn, but also more recently, Grove Garage.

The Greyhound

A trade list of about 1800 mentions, 'The Greyhound now part of Fleece.' If one faces the Fleece today and ignores what was once The Sun it is possible to see two distinct buildings. But which was The Fleece and which was The Greyhound is not known.

The Black Horse

One of the oldest inns in Cirencester, the Black Horse was first mentioned as early as 1674, and mentioned again in an abstract of title dated 1741. In 1794 a meeting was held at the inn to decide upon 'Rules and Orders for a Friendly Society or Ringing Clubb held at the Black Horse, Cirencester.' Friendly Societies are still in existence in the town today but what was the Ringing Club? By 1829 Cripps the brewer had purchased The Black Horse from a man called Stevens for the sum of £350 and an advertisement in 1882 by the landlord, Thomas Mann, says 'Cripps & Co's Old & Bitter Beers and Porter. Mann's Mild a speciality'. It seems odd that Cripps allowed the sale of beer on the premises other than of their own brewing. Cripps must surely have brewed mild beer along with their other varieties. During the same year, 1882, a G. Mann was brewing beer at The Plough Inn, Stratton but Mann was also the name of a national brewer and this brewer is the most likely. There is no evidence of a brewer or brew house at The Black Horse.

Along with several other public houses in the town, renewal of the Black Horse licence was refused by the Compensation Authority and in March 1922 the Black Horse was closed. The Inland Revenue, after the appeals awarded compensation of £970. The neighbouring King's Arms closed in 1924. Part of the King's Arms was sold and converted into shops. Old Cirencestrians may remember Mr Green and his daughter in their fruit and vegetable shop there. The other part of the pub combined with the Black Horse to form enlarged premises, which opened in 1926 under the name The Black Horse Commercial Hotel. The first landlord of the new establishment was Mr W.G. Thornton, mentioned in a directory of 1926. Life at the Black Horse carried on quietly and calmly until, in August 1933, when a ghost appeared! According to *The Cotswold Post* in the summer of that year a lady was staying at the inn

The Black Horse, Castle Street.

when she suddenly awoke with a start and 'heard a scuffling noise coming from a corner of the room and saw the figure of an old woman with an evil expression on her face'. The lady was dressed in what looked like seventeenth-century clothing, a beige coloured dress and a white frilly mobcap. The poor guest on seeing the apparition approaching her bed screamed, and at this the old lady vanished into thin air. The next morning she told the astonishing tale to the landlord who was somewhat sceptical, imagining the lady to have had a bad dream. But on examining the room he noticed on a pane in the window the letter 'W' and 'John' inscribed on the glass. This inscription appeared to go under the lead surrounding the pane so could not have been written without first removing the pane. The landlord swore that the message was not there the previous night and that

73

The Ship Inn, Market Place.

nobody could have tampered with the glass. One attempt to explain this ghostly event ran like this: In the seventeenth century, treasure had been hidden in the house (probably during the Civil War) and when in 1930 alterations were being carried out on the property the old lady returned fearing the treasure would be disturbed and tried to find a safer place to hide it. There were no further recorded sightings of a ghost at the Black Horse, neither has the treasure been found!

Another claim to fame by the Black Horse, though not nearly as exciting, was when an illustration of the inn appeared on a set of cigarette cards published by W.D. & H.O. Wills. Successive inn signs at the hostelry have shown the changing uses of the horse: the oldest I have seen was of a cart horse, the next a hunter and fairly recently a polo pony has been used – all black, of course. The Black Horse is still very much alive, situated in Castle Street opposite the General Post Office.

The Ship

Title deeds for The Ship date from 1784, but when it was first called The Ship is not known. It is not shown on the town map of 1795, nor is it mentioned in the list of around 1800. The earliest-known date as a public house is in a directory of 1820 – 'Mary Tombs, Victualler, the Ship Inn, Dyer Street.'

By 1822 it was under the control of Messrs Cripps Byrch & Co (Cripps Brewery). The Ship had its fair share of licensees including Joseph Boulton, first mention 1847, last mention 1854, the name Boulton is not uncommon among Cirencester licensees. In 1846 the lease of the Ship Inn was taken up by Cripps Byrch at a ground rent of £2 twice a year. Not much is known of life at the Ship, no village carrier seems to have called there, no club or society seems to have met there. Life went on quietly until 1891 when in June of that year the Licensing Authorises refused to renew the licence, the rateable value being £16 per year. The Ship was

not mentioned in the directory of 1891. The building was demolished in about 1897. Scotford Harmer in 1912, said of the Ship, 'On the site of two modern villas now standing (now next to Argos), there was the Ship Inn which had been a fine old building with stone gables and moulded windows and doorway.' At the time of demolition the massive nail-studded oak door bore the carved date 1688. With a description like that it seems a pity the building was not spared for us today, and what happened to the door? Of course the date does not mean the inn was in existence at that time but one interesting possibility is that previously it bore a different name before changing to the Ship, but what?

The Bell

The earliest record of The Bell is from 1540. In his article *Cirencester Past and Present*, Scotford Harmer says The Bell was formerly in Cricklade Street next to the-then Cripps Brewery (now Brewery Court). The hop store of the brewery was the music or assembly rooms of The Bell, circular marks in the ceiling still indicate the position of a pipe organ. In a booklet issued by the brewery in the 1930s there is a photograph of a black and white building entitled The Old Bell Yard showing an entrance into Cricklade Street. The Bell is mentioned in a document dated 1747 and in another one of 1792, by which date the name Cripps appears for the first time. Presumably as Cripps acquired more licensed premises the brewery expanded to meet the demands. All traces of the Old Bell disappeared when this part of Cricklade Street was redeveloped into shops and flats in the 1950s.

The town map of 1795 shows The Bell on the corner of Castle Street and Cricklade Street. The handwritten list of around 1800 gives the address as Cricklade Ward. The terms 'street' and 'ward' were both in use during the first half of the nineteenth century and before and can cause some confusion. The Cirencester Town Map of 1855, for example, shows the part of Castle Street

The Bell Inn.

nearest to the Market Place was not all in Castle Ward, but depending on which side of the street, either in Cricklade Ward or Gosditch Ward. There is a drawing of The Bell sited at the corner of Cricklade Street and Castle Street dated 1820 with the shape of a bell on the wall facing Cricklade Street. In 1847 John Turner was the landlord, address Cricklade Street, but by 1852 William Mills the landlord in Castle Street. It was at about this time, 1855, that The Bell was rebuilt. *The Gloucester Journal* of 1 October 1855 reported as follows: 'A peculiar case of litigation has occurred which has caused much conversation and some interest. On rebuilding the Old Bell it was found necessary to carry up a certain chimney in a safe and careful manner, that an attic crowning the premises of Misses Parsons in Castle Street should be invaded to obtain privilege, the Messrs Cripps & Co of the Brewery offered £60. The fair occupants thinking this was too little and stating £110 their ultimatum. A court case followed in which various counsel were engaged by both sides. The eventual outcome was that £60 was a fair offer and that the Misses Parsons should pay the expenses which it is supposed will amount to rather more than the sum offered!'

The Corinium Lodge of Oddfellows met at The Bell in February 1922. At some time between the wars a room at The Bell was used by a boxer for training purposes but unfortunately no further information about this has come to hand.

For most of the first half of the last century the name Sweeting was connected with The Bell. Mr J. Sweeting was landlord from 1912-27 and from then on until 1940 (the date of the last town directory, due to the outbreak of war) W. Sweeting was in charge.

The Bell ceased to be a public house from about 1957. The large bell motif in bas relief on the corner of the building has been preserved and the premises are now occupied by a firm of estate agents known as 'At the Sign of the Bell', ensuring that a once-prominent public house is remembered.

P.A.T Griffiths

Market forces

After the 1914-18 war many ex-servicemen returned home to find themselves unemployed and in order to help these men the Government asked local authorities to provide smallholdings so that they could grow food for their families. In 1919 the Women's Institute was asked if it would help by selling surplus produce from these small holdings and allotments and as a result of this request the first WI market opened in Lewes, Sussex - it is still trading today.

Soon WI markets were opening throughout the country and in 1932 the National Federation of Women's Institutes was asked by the Ministry of Agriculture to help to feed the nation by increasing the amount of home produced food.

The result was the formation of a National Markets Department whose aim was to increase the number of WI markets. This effort was helped by a special grant from the Carnegie UK Trust which was given on a reducing scale until finally the Markets Department could finance its own organisation.

In return the Trust asked the NFWI to make membership of the Markets open to non-WI members, men and women, and this has been the policy since 1932.

WI markets were well established when the Second World War started and were able to play a part in helping to make each parish self-supporting as well as sending fresh fruit and vegetables to the towns. In 1995, WI markets became completely independent of the NFWI, and WI Country Markets Ltd was formed to administer the network of WI Markets. This change was made to protect the charitable status of the WI.

WI markets are run as non-profit-making businesses with roughly 90% of income being returned to the producers and the remaining 10% covering rental, insurance and a quota to WI Country Markets Ltd.

There are about 500 WI Markets throughout England, Wales and the Channel Islands and around 13,000 producers. In 2001 the annual turnover was over £11 million. Each market is run by a committee with a chairman, treasurer and secretary elected from among the shareholders and the stalls are manned by shareholders. A controller is appointed to look after the organisation and standards of the market. These are some of the goods you may find at Cirencester WI Market: bread and cakes, tray bakes and pastries, savouries, jams and marmalades, pickles and chutneys, honey, eggs, crafts, cut flowers, fruit, plants and vegetables. Cirencester WI market was the first to be set up in Gloucestershire and opened for business in September 1933. Since then it has been held on Fridays in the vicinity of the marketplace.

For nearly fifty years it held prime position at the head of the marketplace. It may have been the prime position but the conditions were rather primitive. For thirty-three years produce was sold from a hut before a canvas-covered stall was provided. From there it moved to the Crown Hotel yard where it stayed for three years and then, after a period at the Golden Cross, the market came to rest at Bingham House – a far cry from those early days of open markets. Old records tell of great discomfort – leaking roofs, insufficient shelter and a Tilly lamp to provide a little warmth in the hut!

Over the years many changes have taken place regarding the sale of food – vegetables and fruit used to be brought to market in bulk and weighed on the spot; plants were brought in large boxes, dug out and wrapped in newspaper. Now all baked goods, fruit and most vegetables have to be pre-packed and labelled and plants are well-grown in pots. Cirencester WI market has survived all the changes and challenges and is proud of its history. It continues to offer its customers a wide variety of good home produce as well as opportunities for new producers to become members of this great market network.

Pauline Trevallion

8 All Things Bright and Beautiful

Angel heralds

Angels are ever-present in the church of St John Baptist, Cirencester. They peer out from amongst the darkened timbers of the roofs, look down from the stone vaults, willingly submit to be burdened by heavy roof posts, stand proudly around the tops of lofty piers and appear in glowing colours in many of the windows. While some of those depicted in stained glass are cherubims from the upper echelons of the angel hierarchy, the others only claim is to be members of the heavenly host. To be in the presence of so many celestial inhabitants is, of course, reassuring, though on close examination, it will be found that these angels are not lauding their Creator but paying homage to those benefactors, whose liberality made the buildings of this splendid church possible.

Twenty-six of these shield bearing angels look down from the piers supporting the nave, rebuilt in the period 1514-30. Their prototypes adorn the piers and walls of the Trinity Chapel attached to the north side of the church and completed in the mid-fifteenth century. Few of these angels' shields retain their painted armorial bearings. In the nave many of the coats of arms, although frequently repainted, have survived. Not all of the heraldry dates back to the Middle Ages. The arms of the bishoprics of Gloucester, Worcester and Bristol were added in the nineteenth century as were those of Cirencester town.

The shields of ancient origin fall into several categories. Firstly there are the ecclesiastical patrons. The arms of Rowthall impaling the bishopric of Durham remind us of John Leland's comments, made when he visited Cirencester in 1542. The bishop, who was born and bred in the town, promised much but, prevented by death in 1522, gave nothing. The other church dignitary is John Hakeboum, Abbot of the Augustinian Abbey, which stood a few yards north-east of the parish church. His generosity is suggested by two shields bearing his initials, one with the arms of the abbey, the other with a mitre and pastoral staff. These shields are a reminder of the great wealth of the abbey, which was currently rebuilding its own nave.

The next group consists of local nobility and gentry. These include members of the Berkeley family, donors who died sometime before building work commenced on the nave. There is also Sir John Hungerford and his wife from Down Ampney. He left £3 to the fabric fund, while she donated her best velvet gown to be remade into vestments. Sir Robert Morton, nephew of the notorious Cardinal Morton is probably also represented. His donation is not recorded but his mother left £6 13s 4d on her death in 1485 to defray the cost of building works. Sir William Compton from Warwickshire at one time steward of the abbey's manors and Sir Edmund Tame, son of the builder of Fairford church and also a steward of the abbey are both commemorated though their bequests are not known. Another shield probably refers to a donation of £20 left by R. Osmunde. Two ladies are among the benefactors – Dame

Arms of Berkeley & Beverstone.

Arms of Compton.

Shield of Henry Topper.

Alice Pratt, who died in 1529 and by the terms of her husband's will left the residue of their estate to the church. Leland makes reference to Alice Aveling, who was the aunt of Bishop Rowthall of Durham. She had given a 100 marks towards the cost of building the south porch and her shield is on the south aisle.

The great churches, which arose to grace towns and villages in the Cotswold during the late Middle Ages are often referred to as Wool Churches, the supposition being that they were paid for out of the profits of the thriving wool trade. The benefactors so far mentioned were not obviously associated with this trade. However, the abbey at Cirencester had extensive flocks of sheep and Sir Edmund Tame's father, John, was a notable wool merchant. Our third category of benefactor, the tradesmen, does include a wool merchant.

Arms of Durham.

Angel with blank shield, c. 1450.

A shield with 'RR' and a merchant's mark probably refers to Robert Rycardes a clothier, who was also bailiff of Cirencester. He died in 1518 leaving £20 to the building of the middle aisle. Adjacent to this shield is one inscribed H.T. with a merchant's mark, which could be that of Henry Tapper, a grocer who died in 1530. By that time the structure of the nave would have been completed so he donated £10 for fittings, including the rood loft, the organ, hangings of the high altar and vestments for the Lady Chapel. He also left a legacy of £20 towards the cost of new seating. Another shield has on it 'I.B.' along with the banner of St John Baptist. This could be for John Bennett, who died in 1497 and whose brass is now in the Lady Chapel. At the western end of the south aisle are three further shields probably related to

merchant benefactors. One with a merchant's mark, two with the banner of St John.

The message conveyed by these angel heralds raises a number of queries. It provides limited support for the suggestion that the nave rose on the backs of sheep. Some of those associated with the shields died long before the nave was commenced, though it is possible that payment was made following the death of the relics. There is evidence that a few of the legacies were used for work not associated with the nave, while the bishop of Durham apparently is there on false pretences. Besides, are all of these winged beings really little angels? Some have headdresses of a martial form, while one bears a striking resemblance to Sir George Gilbert Scott, the architect responsible for the nineteenth-century restoration of the nave.

Jim Thompson

Shield of John Bennett.

Songs of praise

The Choral Society's own archives go back only as far as 1937, but our discovery in 2000 of the gravestone of Richard Mann, in the parish churchyard, indicated that Cirencester Choral Society existed in 1869. This triggered our researches which reveal that it was founded in 1863 and, with a few interruptions, continues to this day. Its members, sometimes numbering over a hundred, represent the largest organised participatory activity in the Cotswold district.

The founding of the Society is closely linked, through its early conductors, with the revival of choral music in the Anglican Church influenced by the Oxford Movement and the Cambridge equivalent – the Camden Society. Before we can describe those links we must first introduce some of the national personages involved.

Two of the leading lights in the Oxford Movement were the Keble brothers from Fairford. John, after whom Keble College was named, retired to Eastleach; and Thomas became Vicar of Bisley.

St Mark's College, Chelsea, had been founded to train teachers who would also become parish organists and choirmasters. In charge of music and also Precentor in the chapel was the Revd Thomas Helmore who in 1846 was additionally appointed Master of the Children of the Chapel Royal. (The children are still seen on Royal occasions resplendent in their scarlet and gold tunics.) Helmore took the children daily to supplement the choir at St Mark's and involved them in various other events including the four performances of Elijah under Mendelssohn's own baton in 1847.

Thomas Helmore's younger brother, Frederick was invited by Prince Albert to become his personal choirmaster, which involved training choirs drawn from the staff of Windsor Castle and Buckingham Palace. Frederick spent most of his life travelling the country, training parish choirs, starting public choral classes and organising choral festivals. At one such festival, at Withyam in Kent, his brother brought the Children of the Chapel Royal to assist. Frederick Helmore earned the sobriquet 'The Musical Missionary' but his itinerant lifestyle led to little being now known about him and what happened to his choral classes – with one notable exception.

Up the road from Chelsea, Thomas Helmore's associate from Oxford, the Revd Frederick Gore Ouseley, opened the church of St Barnabas in 1849 as a mission in the then slum area of Pimlico. Being steeped in the Oxford Movement he introduced high church ritual and trained an excellent choir. However, opponents of this 'Roman ritualism' rioted at the church and the vacillating Bishop of London closed it and sacked the choir. Ouseley, a very wealthy man, housed the choir in Buckinghamshire until he had built and opened in 1856 the church and college of St Michael's at Tenbury, Worcestershire. Thomas Helmore provided assistance at the opening service – again with the children including a brilliant young treble soloist, Arthur S. Sullivan. If you have stayed with us through this brief history lesson we can now come to Cirencester.

Records exist of Cirencester Harmonic Society, founded in 1776, which gave performances at the Woodhouse in Cirencester Park. We believe that this was a gentleman's glee club and do not claim it as a forerunner of Cirencester Choral Society. The Revd Thomas Keble brought Frederick Helmore, 'The Musical Missionary', to Bisley in 1862, no doubt to train choirs in the five Chapels of Ease he had built in neighbouring villages. Helmore also advertised choral classes in neighbouring towns, and the one in Cirencester he named Cirencester Choral Society. The first class was held in the Assembly Room at the King's Head on Tuesday 6 October 1863. True to his missionary intent, Helmore admitted members of church choirs at half price or less. Tuesday remains the Society's rehearsal evening to this day.

In April 1864 Helmore announced rehearsals, intending to lead to the first performance in Cirencester of Handel's *Messiah,* He was over-optimistic. The Society's first concert on 12 May 1864, mainly to an audience of the members' friends and relations, was a mixed programme but did include some excerpts from *Messiah.* Soon after this, Frederick Helmore moved to Devon from whence he continued his chosen nomadic life. His contribution to the spread of singing throughout the country, not only in churches, must have been enormous. How many of his choral classes still continue as choral societies?

In October 1864 Cirencester Choral Society restarted classes now under the

Oratorio programme, Cirencester Choral Society, 1867.

direction of Richard Mann aged about twenty-eight. We know nothing of his date and place of birth or of his parents. Two brothers attended his funeral and he left everything (about £200) to his brother George. He had been one of the Children of the Chapel Royal under Thomas Helmore, had sung *Elijah* under Mendelssohn and had been a lay clerk in the choir at St Michael's, Tenbury. It is probable that he sang at the festival at Withyam (an early contact with Frederick Helmore) and that he developed a friendship with a fellow chorister, Arthur Sullivan. At Tenbury, the lay clerks were required to teach in the schoolroom so his own education must have extended beyond his time as one of the Children. Could this have been also with Thomas Helmore at St Mark's, Chelsea? In that case it would be easy to explain how Ouseley, in recruiting lay clerks-cum-teachers for Tenbury, would have accepted Mann on the recommendation of his friend Thomas Helmore.

We do not know what brought Mann to Gloucestershire but the suggestion that, like Frederick Helmore, the Revd Thomas Keble recruited him seems plausible. He also took over, from Helmore, the baton of the Stroud and Cirencester Choral Societies. In 1865 he was appointed Choirmaster to the Choral Union in the Rural Deanery which involved training village choirs – much as Frederick Helmore had done.

In his first two seasons Mann and the Choral Society gave several concerts with a mixed programme of songs, glees and choruses from oratorios. By 1867 the Society was ready for its first major oratorio and Haydn's *Creation* was performed in the Corn Hall on 6 May with full band and professional soloists. The chorus numbered over a hundred and the hall was 'filled by a delighted audience' including 'Lord Bathurst and members of nearly all the leading families of the district'. Unfortunately Richard Mann's health had begun to fail and Edward Brind conducted the concert.

The Vicar of Cirencester at this time was the Revd Canon William Powell. He had tried to introduce High Church ritual and music but was frustrated by the unsuitability of the church and its organ, by elements of the congregation who rioted and by his organist, J.W. Mills, who refused to play High Church music. By 1865, however, Powell was ready to take the bull by the horns and Sir George Gilbert Scott was engaged to refurbish the church. Gray & Davison installed a new organ, and Mills was sacked. What happened to the rioters is not recorded.

Richard Mann's ill health prevented him from carrying out the arduous travelling necessitated by his Choral Union appointment and he resigned. Fortunately for all parties Canon Powell was able to offer him the job, from which the disobedient Mr Mills had

been ejected, so Mann trained the choir and played the organ for the Grand Reopening Service on 27 November 1867.

Richard Mann was able to continue with the Choral Society and, in May 1868 they performed *The May Queen* by Sterndale Bennett. This was in front of 'a crowded and fashionable audience including the Earl Bathurst and a party from Oakley House and Mr and Mrs Master from the Abbey'. The applause was 'frequent and hearty'. In December of that year Richard Mann conducted a Ballad Concert. By then he had moved to a room above Harmer's printing office in the Market Place – now the premises of Sahara ladies' fashions.

Early in 1869 Mann began rehearsals for Handel's *Judas Maccabaeus* but his health was failing and Edward Brind again conducted the performance. The Revd Sir Frederick Gore Ouseley came to visit Mann's sickbed and all the members of the Choral Society signed the following letter to him:

Cirencester, 9th April 1869
Dear Mr Mann
We the undersigned members of the Cirencester Choral Society, beg to express our grief at your severe illness and to offer you our heartfelt sympathy.

It may afford you a moment's gratification if we also take this opportunity of saying how much we feel indebted to you for your kind instruction and your unvarying and patient perseverance with us.

That your sufferings may be tempered to you as far as possible is the earnest prayer of Your very sincere friends.

He replied:

My Dear Friends
I am sorry my communication to you must be short, but I feel bound to write it myself, and my strength is not great. How can I thank you properly for your kind expression of

sympathy? God has been very good to me and I suffer little from pain. The periodical meeting of the class has always been one of the bright spots in my week's work – you know this better than I can tell you. When the pain has held me your bright faces have made me forget all. I shall think of you all on Thursday – you must do better than you have done before. With all best wishes, and a request that you will give me your prayers.

I am, Yours most gratefully,

Richard Mann

Market Place, Cirencester, April 13th 1869.

Richard Mann died on 29 April 1869. Canon Powell took the funeral service assisted by the Revd John Hampton who had been Mann's choirmaster at Tenbury. Mann himself composed much of the music sung at the service and which continued to the graveside. *The Standard* published a glowing obituary, fulsome even for those days. His friends published in his memory a book of Seven Songs composed by Mann and 140 were subscribed at the then high price of 10s 6d each. The list of subscribers features most of the great and good of this area as well as Tenbury and also includes Arthur Sullivan and Thomas Helmore and his family.

On visiting the church of St Michael's at Tenbury, we were staggered to discover a stained glass window with a plaque containing the words:

'In Memory of Mr Richard Mann a Member of the Choir of this Church from 1857 to 1864, this Window was given by many of his Friends, July 1875'.

What a privilege to have been one of the many friends of this young man, but of whom we know so little. What an impression he must have made for this window to have been given six years after his death.

By 1869 Cirencester Choral Society had survived its difficult birth thanks to the two remarkable men who were its first conductors,

Memorial to Richard Mann 1869.

both of whom were dedicated to music in church rather than concert hall. Except for a few brief interludes, the Society continues to the present day. Richard Mann was followed by Ernest Cockton who had been assistant to the great music teacher, John Hullah, and he was succeeded by Edward Brind, who had taught music to the young Hubert Parry – but that is another story.

Lorna Lane and Tim Page

Memorial window to Richard Mann.

Holy Trinity church

In 1841 the population of Cirencester was 6,000, and the parish church in the Market Place was only able to minister to just over 1,500 people in enclosed pews. The Vicar of Cirencester at the time was the Revd (later Canon) William Powell who found a solution to this problem by making it possible for at least half of the local population, rather than just almost a third to be able to worship by the building of a new church planned to be located at Watermoor in the south of the town. The architect assigned to draw up the plans was Sir George Gilbert-Scott. The site of one and a half acres was offered by Henry George fourth Earl Bathurst, the grant of the land to the church was made by Mr Joseph Randolph Mullings, lessee of the land and owner of Watermoor House nearby. The

The church choir 1952-1954.

public was invited to give subscriptions and collection books were issued to some of the leading church folk. In all £6,000 was raised and of that £1,200 was invested in the purchase of the adjacent field – then known as the Paddock together with the buildings and cottage.

On St David's Day in 1847 the foundation stone was laid. In a special ceremony the children of the Blue and Yellow Schools walked over the stones to impress upon their memories the place of the Mother Church, similar to the ritual of 'Beating the Bounds'.

The church was designed and its construction supervised by Sir George Gilbert-Scott. It was built by Mr Bridges, a local builder of that time in the style of Gothic revival. The stone used for the outside came from a quarry in the London Road, and Bath stone was used for the interior. Throughout the building phase, water was obtained from a well, which

was dug, and the water was pumped with a pump, which still exists to this day.

And so the church was built for the costly sum of £5,000 and took four years to build, at this time without either spire or a complete south side. During the construction phase, one workman lost his life when hit by falling scaffolding. The water table is not very far below the surface in this area and this is the reason to this day, why no burials are permitted at Holy Trinity Watermoor.

Inside, the church has great appeal, highlighted by triple lancets above a coloured and gilded reredos also designed by Sir George Gilbert-Scott. A Polish man, E. Geflowski made the reredos and stone carvings; he went on to become famous for the reredos at All Souls College Oxford and the one in the parish church in Cirencester. Altogether he made some 1,000 carvings in Holy Trinity for the grand sum of a mere £56.

Messrs J. Taylor of Loughborough installed the bells over several years starting in 1887 and the last one in 1901. Fine iron gates were located at the front door to a design by Mr Christopher Bishop (architect), a later working design and ironwork was carried out by Mr Michael Roberts, an art ironworker of Miserden.

The Consecration of the Holy Trinity church at Watermoor took place on 6 November 1851. It should have been conducted by the Lord Bishop of Gloucester and Bristol (The Rt Revd Dr D.H. Monk) but owing to illness was conducted by the Bishop of Llandaff (The Rt Revd Dr A. Oliphant. After the service of consecration, matins was sung by Canon Powell led by choristers of Gloucester Cathedral and aided by boys of the Blue and Yellow Schools. It was indeed a memorable day for Cirencester and it was made certain that no child should ever be allowed to forget the day. It is believed that over 420 school children of the parish were regaled, at a dinner later that day, with a plentiful supply of roast beef and plum puddings that had been made by the ladies of the town. After the consecration, work began to assemble all the necessary additions to the church for regular use by the congregation. There were neither vestries nor scarcely any interior decorations. Even the worshippers were summoned to church by a cracked gong pending a full peal of bells in later years. Many donors came forward and soon the church was resplendent with spire, south aisle – and a primitive heating system. The system was upgraded in 1860 and still uses the under-floor ducts to this day as well as more modern radiators. The main reredos was erected in 1879 at a cost of £500, which included tiling the sanctuary floor and enlarging the altar, the money having been provided by the ladies of the congregation. The pulpit was designed with open steps by Sir George Gilbert-Scott but after the Second World War, when greater use was made of visiting and retired clergy, the steps were considered dangerous and so, using generous donations by, Mr Billy Hall in memory of his wife, and the South Cerney Angling Club in memory of Mr George Hester, an oak and wrought iron handrail was made by J. Hall Blacksmith of Quern's Lane Cirencester was installed.

A small recess was made in the wall to the south side of the Lady Chapel and turned into a lockable aumbry in which to keep the reserved Sacrament. These Sacraments were reserved for house communions for the sick and housebound and other visits. An electric aumbry lamp is always alight when the sacraments are in the aumbry. This replaced the sole surviving oil lamp that hung from the centre beam of the chapel. The other six oil lamps are reputed to be adorning various churches throughout the diocese.

The lectern was donated by members of the congregation as was the original altar cross, in memory of loved ones and about the same time the pulpit was built from funds received from a collection taken amongst the scholars of Cirencester Ladies' School. A lady whose husband had died in a rail accident provided the font, and a brass cover for it was given by Mrs Weldon in memory of her daughter, Mrs Charles Sewell. Sometime during the 1940s this cover fell from its roof support and slightly damaged the font and its supporting pillars. The broken beam is still visible in the roof above the font to this day. The church hall was added in 1971-72 when the Mission Room on Chesterton Lane was demolished, to make way for relief road. The Garden of Remembrance was created in the mid 1970s.

The windows are one of the most interesting features of the church. There are a total of sixteen and each one has a story to tell. Each window is numbered from W1 to W16 and a chart showing the story and details of each window will be available in the church for visitors.

In a cabinet below the windows W1 and W2

A wedding at Watermoor church in the late 1940s.

(to the left of the main door on entry, the Book of Remembrance was installed at the same time as the font. The font is made of Derbyshire marble and was obtained from St Asaph's Cathedral by The Revd John Stevens. In 1972, through a legacy in memory of a local farmers family, the two stained glass windows were installed as a pair. They were designed and made by Lawrence Lee of Penshurst in Kent and installed by a local man, Joe Barnard. The artist was asked to design the windows with the theme of Birth and Baptism, Death and the Book of Remembrance. These two new and complex windows follow the traditional style of depicting a biblical story, the more one studies the more one discovers. The Old and the New Testaments have been deliberately mixed in both windows suggesting the continuity of God's working in history. The underlying structure of the windows is triangular (Holy Trinity) and circular (eternity).

The earliest window in the south sanctuary was purchased from Tetbury Parish, by the Revd William Powell, using public donations, and probably dates from before 1850, but is almost certainly by Michael O'Connor, the rose window (W3) over the organ dates from 1853 and was also by the O'Connors. Windows 4,5 and 6, (the Tetbury window) also windows 13,14,15 and 16 are all by the Michael and Arthur O'Connor – father and son partnership, working from Bristol then London. Windows 7, 8, 9, 11, 12, are all by John Hardman of Birmingham, who worked closely with Pugin and in truly Gothic Revival Style. W10 remains as plain glass. More details of the other windows in the church can be seen on a leaflet in the nave of the church at the information desk.

Eight bells, make up the peal of bells, each of which has a 70 ft rope. The bells were installed on wooden and metal frames in the belfry in 1887 to 1901. Six of them were re-hung in 1989 using money left by Mrs Dorothy Minnis. The sacring bell was installed in 1932 being donated by Miss Lawrence. The foundation bell, the tenor, weighing 20 cwt, was given in 1887 by the Misses Brown of Further Barton, Cirencester; two years later they gave two more bells. Another two bells were given by Miss Esther Young and another by Mr Thomas Smith. By 1901 the octave was completed by the addition of two more bells given in memory of Mr Thomas Lewis by his widow and family. They were all cast by Messrs Taylor of Loughborough and are reputed to be one of the best peals for their weight. They were chosen to represent Gloucestershire in a *Faith in the West* programme broadcast by the BBC on the 3 July 1953.

The clock and chimes were presented by Mr Thomas Lewis in 1899 and were dedicated on the Trinity Sunday of that year. They were manufactured by Messrs Smith of Derby at a cost of £140. The spire, that stands out clearly as a landmark for miles around, was added in 1852 at the expense of the Hon. William Lennox Bathurst. Its height is 150 ft and it has lightning conductor rods placed on it for protection from electric storms. The spire had to be repaired when lightning struck it a few years ago and traces of the repair are still visible in the top 30 ft of the stonework. Of interest, while the scaffolding was in position a vandal gained access to the spire and, having taken off the hour hand from the clock, was seen waving it about at the top of the church. The hands are now back in position and the clock keeps good time.

The organ was neither provided nor contemplated when the church was dedicated in 1851. Until 1863 the singing in the church was sometimes without accompaniment and sometimes with the aid of boy instrumentalists of the Powell's school in Gloucester Street. With the help of adult members of the parish church choir, the pupils of Powell's School took turns in coming to Watermoor. In 1863 a harmonium was provided and in 1867

Bishop & Starr built the first organ at a cost of £250. By 1892 even this organ was considered inadequate and a specification was drawn up by Messrs Bishop & Son, for a larger organ more in keeping with the size of the church.

The new organ was built by the following year at a cost of £500 and incorporated many of the original pipes. In January 1963 the organ was due for a full restoration which was completed by Palm Sunday in April 1963, and later in 1999 further restoration work was undertaken at a cost of £28,000.

The Mission Room (now long gone) was built at the lower end of Chesterton Lane in 1893-94. Workers from the adjacent Midland Railway at Watermoor station regularly used it, many of whom were itinerant. The railway line ran from Andoversford to Swindon Old Town station and quite often men from the railway works used the Mission Room for 'Mission' meetings, refreshments and as a reading room for talks and lectures. Other organisations in the town used the Mission Room for cubs, scouts and guides, church social functions, weddings, receptions and birthday parties. It could accommodate up to seventy people for these events.

In 2001, approximately six months before the celebration of the 150th anniversary of the church a vandal set fire to the West door causing considerable damage to the building and contents. The damage was covered by insurance and, thankfully, was made good before the celebratory event later that year. This involved the complete manufacture of a new door. The whole of the interior of the church had to be re-decorated. Fortunately the fire, having been discovered in time, was rapidly put out, but any delay could have meant a much more unfortunate result. Of interest, there was not a single service missed during the whole of this event.

There are many more tales about the church that are further explained in the booklet *The 150th Anniversary of Holy Trinity Church Watermoor* which is obtainable from the Cornerstone Bookshop in Gosditch Street. In 2001 the church celebrated its 150th Anniversary. A whole week of events took place around the 6 November including a pageant by children of Watermoor School. It was filmed by BBC Television and included a re-enactment of the Consecration of the Church by children acting as the Bishop of Llandaff and Earl Bathurst. Syd Little of the Little and Large team came and gave an excellent concert and discussion of his reformed life, and concerts and a dinner were held to celebrate the anniversary. A plan is in place to create an archive of all the events concerned with the 150th Anniversary in boxes that will be stored for use by the committee who will arrange the 200th Anniversary in 2051. This involves putting a time capsule describing events and living conditions of this time for the use of future generations of worshippers at this wonderful and most beautiful church.

Tony Clack

Defeating the demon drink

The Temperance Hall in Thomas Street has a chequered history. Born out of the fears of widespread drunkenness which followed the easing of duties on beer in 1830, the temperance movement, in the South of England grew rapidly, with the enthusiastic support of the influential middle class, especially in the nonconformist chapels. In Cirencester, the temperance pioneers were all Quakers and when, in 1845, the opportunity arose to buy up a brewery opposite the Friends Meeting House, together with the nearby Hole in the Wall public house, Christopher Bowly, a prominent Quaker and local philanthropist, saw a way of demonstrating the victory of sobriety over intemperance, in bricks and mortar.

He purchased the site and, at a cost of £2,126, constructed a Victorian Gothic building which was the first Temperance Hall in the West of England. The Hall could seat 600, including the gallery, and the floorboards were made from brewers' vats – trodden underfoot by the righteous, this would be another symbol of the defeat of 'demon drink'. It opened on Christmas Day 1846, with a grand ceremony and public tea, when Bowly declared that he wished it to be used primarily for the advancement of temperance but also 'the promotion of all benevolent and philanthropic objects… to the spread of useful knowledge and, indeed, to any purpose which is calculated to increase the welfare and happiness of my fellow man'.

In the following year, a trust of fourteen fellow Quakers was set up to administer the hall, appoint a caretaker (the first was Mary Hewer) and handle the finances – any profits over £100 were to be donated to

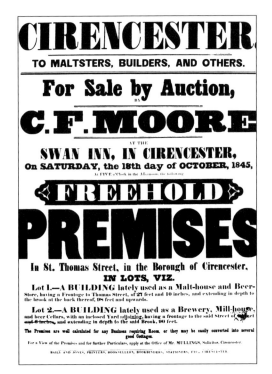

Property sale poster, 1845.

Temperance Hall, Cirencester, 1846.

temperance causes. The trust first met after Bowly's death in 1851 and by that time The Temperance Hall was already well established in its role as the focus for local activity. Initially, this meant the encouragement of 'moderation' in drinking – indeed, one trustee described himself as a 'wine merchant' – but, in common with the national picture, 'temperance' soon became 'total abstinence'. Some of Bowly's associates were suspicious of the extrovert emotionalism of teetotal meetings addressed by reformed drunkards, which seemed more like music hall turns than educational experiences but, especially under the influence of local Congregationalists, more forthright views and less squeamish approaches developed.

In the middle of the nineteenth century, the Thomas Street hall was the home for all shades of temperance opinion. The Cirencester Temperance Society organised regular meetings with prominent speakers and its annual Tea Meeting celebrated the opening of the hall and aimed to achieve maximum publicity for the cause. In 1851, Samuel Bowly spoke to a well-filled hall under a banner with the slogan 'Because of Drunkenness the Land Mourneth' and, probably more in hope than expectation, called on Queen Victoria and Prince Albert to 'sign the pledge'. These meetings lacked the fire of the Cirencester Total Abstinence Society, where the atmosphere was more like revivalist religious gatherings and the intention was to provide alternative entertainment to the public house. Temperance hymns, like 'The Day We Signed the Pledge' and 'Begone Strong Drink' were sung and, together with readings and recitations, a mass version of the family 'soiree' was produced to prove 'the compatibility of temperance principles with rational enjoyment'. This approach was to be the one which dominated in local temperance as the century wore on.

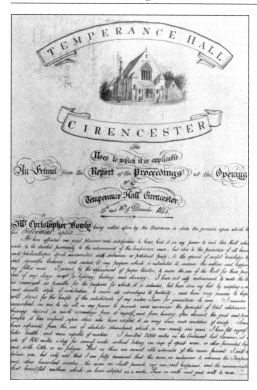

Extract from opening speech, 1846.

In its heyday, Cirencester temperance spawned a wide variety of other organisations. By the late 1850s, regular meetings of the Band of Hope attracted 'a crowded attendance of children' and a decade later there were 400 on the books and a drum and fife band was started. Temperance discussion classes were started in 1868. In 1871, The Order of Good Templars established its first lodge, with an inauguration tea attracting 200 people, although the absence of many of the 'old temperance reformers' was noted, a sign of the growing discomfort of the more respectable with some of the new campaigning methods. A branch of the Red Ribbon Army was started in 1882 – the political connotations of its 'Blue Ribbon' counterpart were regarded with some suspicion by local nonconformist Liberals. Despite the diversities within the movement (the Church of England had its own society

View of Thomas Street, 1887.

which met elsewhere and tended to avoid the nonconformist groups), temperance was able to command a good deal of interest and support. When J.B. Gough, a well-known American temperance orator, visited Cirencester, the local newspaper produced a special supplement devoted solely to the meeting. Around 700 were able to get seats, policemen were needed to control the crowds and there was even a black market in tickets. Other gatherings attracted audiences well beyond the hall's capacity and, in 1868,

Samuel Bowly claimed that ten per cent of the town was teetotal. The annual Temperance Fete, held near Pope's Seat in Cirencester Park, brought in over 4,000 people that year and, with regular attendances of 3,000, was said, in 1870 to be 'one of the events of the season', although the introduction of donkey races was the subject of some controversy. There was no shortage of speakers with sound advice for the drinker. In 1852 four 'working men' alluding to the new railways, showed the 'steam could be got up' without the aid of 'artificial stimulants'. Jabez Inward, in a lecture on 'Uncle Tom's Cabin', claimed that the English slave to drink was in a worse condition than the black plantation workers in America. The Revd J.T. Messer, in 1858, was able to claim that 'physical strength is impaired, domestic comfort dissipated and intellectual faculties darkened, the moral powers degraded and prostituted by the use of alcohol'.

The solution seemed to lie in a change in working class drinking habits and attitudes and, from the outset, reformers, like the Bowlys, saw real value in encouraging self help and other 'Victorian values'. The Temperance hall became a centre for lectures and courses on a wide variety of topics. In 1849, Henry Vincent the fiery Chartist orator was the subject of a lively local debate when it was feared that his 'red republican' speech had turned the hall into 'an arena of sedition and irreligion' and had created an atmosphere of 'mental intemperance'.

More in line with the trustees' ideas was the adoption of the hall by the local Mechanics Institute for adult education in the winter months. The founders of the Mechanics Institute were solid 'respectable' men – professional and businessmen and academics from the Royal Agricultural College (begun contemporaneously with Bowly's hall and, for a short time its next-door neighbour in Thomas Street). Their attempt to 'improve'

The Temperance Hall, 1977.

the working classes, however, seems to have been largely unsuccessful. The annual subscription of ten shillings or individual meeting fees of one shilling probably discouraged most working men and the 1852 topics offered, including 'The Life and Character of Alfred the Great', 'The Teaching of Shakespeare' and 'The Uses of Poetry' lacked mass appeal, as did the 1858 lecture on 'The Grandeur, Guilt and Wrongs of Richard III'. Only for novelty evenings could a wider audience be reached, as in February 1859, when the hall was nearly filled for Mr Pumphrey's 'Illustrated View of Egypt and the Holy Land' – shown by means of oxy-hydrogen light. Other formal lecture courses, such as those offered to the Cirencester School of Art by Professor Church of the Royal Agricultural College on inorganic chemistry and, less

The Temperance Hall, 2002.

successfully on agriculture and general science in 1871, were clearly aimed at the already educated, although, in 1880, an exhibition of photographs of the Cathedrals of England, using a 'triplexicon lantern', proved popular.

As a rule, the majority of the poor were untouched by these worthy activities. Even the friendly societies, such as the Foresters, who used the committee room, were aimed at 'a better class' of worker. The original trust deed discouraged overtly political use of the hall but, in addition to Vincent's visit, there were gatherings of a political nature. In 1852, two energetic meetings about the 'Kaffir War' were addressed by David Bowly and the possible calling out of the local militia was discussed. That same militia was entertained at later dates at the hall – in 1852 by lectures on 'Electricity' and 'English History' and, in 1870, by temperance meetings, when it was reported that 'some were inclined to be troublesome'. The Bowly philanthropic interests were also represented by land reform meetings and the 'Workmen's Peace Association', which met in 1872 to condemn the high levels of government expenditure on warfare.

Most of the trustees were Liberal in their politics and in 1878 the hall was let out to Mr Ashley Ponsonby who challenged the Conservatives at the election. Thomas Brewin, secretary to the trustees evidently considered this preferable to the party's former use of tents in the Bull Inn yard for Liberal Campaigns. Having set the precedent, Mr Newcombe, a prominent teetotaller, later used the premises for his initial unsuccessful local election bid.

Earlier, in 1880, Joseph Arch, the Agricultural Labourers' Union leader addressed a meeting demanding the extension of the franchise to farm workers. While the trustees were 'liberal' in their interpretation of the trust deed in politics, they could be less tolerant in religion. A refusal to let the hall to the Unitarians, who wanted to talk about 'free thought' in religion, in 1873, led to a 'public indignation meeting' and the distribution of critical leaflets around the town. With the exception of the Unitarians, many religious groups used the hall and there was always an overlap between temperance and (especially) nonconformist religion, which is reflected in the appearance of the hall. The British and Foreign Bible Society, The Religious Tract Society and The Christian Mutual Improvement Society all used the premises and, in 1880, members of the Roman Catholic Chapel entertained friends to tea. The hall's liveliest period as a religious meeting place was probably in the 1880s when the Salvation Army established its 'barracks' there. From its arrival in September 1881, the new movement was the focus of daily rioting on the streets, often encouraged by local publicans. The police were frequently called to 'unblock' Thomas Street and the new caretaker, the rather inappropriately named Edward Brewer, often had to assist in barring the door to noisy rioters hurling missiles and verbal abuse. Inside, the meetings were equally noisy – so much so that, in l883, the trustees requested the Salvationists to 'discontinue the use of the drum, at least on Sundays'. Worries about major damage to the hall led to the curtailment of meetings for some time.

While the hall had been used for a wide variety of activities, the 1880s saw the start of a long-term decline. Since opening, the nature of its availability prevented the hall from becoming a full public amenity. As early as 1855, the local newspaper commented, that 'however admirable the Temperance Hall is for tea drinking and speech making, it is, owing to the absurd restrictions imposed on its use, rendered useless for other purposes'. The opening of the Corn Hall, in 1862, eventually provided a venue for 'lectures, cheap entertainments and concerts' which were banned from Thomas Street and, while the Temperance Hall remained in demand in the winter months, its popularity diminished, except for meetings directly associated with temperance.

As the nineteenth century drew to a close, even temperance groups began to move away. Increasingly, the Congregationalists took over from the Quakers and meetings took place more frequently at their chapel. By 1900, demand for the hall had almost ceased. Temperance, as a mass movement, was a spent force. In the 1860s meetings regularly filled the hall to capacity but later accounts referred to declining numbers and 'a beggarly display of empty benches'. A decline in the local Quaker population at the same time brought about a crisis in the management of the premises. By 1900 there were only five trustees, mainly from outside Cirencester, and long-term maintenance problems caused major concerns, which were not solved by increasing hire charges to a diminishing number of customers. Three years later, a special meeting was convened to discuss 'the present unsatisfactory position of the charity' and it was decided to let the property to a group representing the Free Church Council at an annual rental of £10. While the Good Templars continued to meet in the committee room, the main hall was difficult to let and the decline continued.

When the agreement with the Free Churches ended in 1910 (the £10 rent was proving difficult to find) a possible new lease of life was offered when Messrs Fowler and Sims announced the opening of the 'People's Electric Theatre'. The cinema had arrived and patrons were promised a good two hours' enjoyment when 'the whole world would be surveyed' – from Monday to Saturday. Alternative 'religious' entertainment was provided on by the 'Pleasant Sunday Afternoon' movement, which, by 1914, was also filling an evening slot.

War brought a change of use and for a while the hall had a role as a military hospital but, despite a short term temperance revival in the 1920s, the future looked grim. The only local trustee in 1924 was J.A. Gillett of the Cirencester grocery firm and the Charity Commission was called in to create a new trust from elected councillors and the Free Churches, following an unsuccessful attempt to sell the property to the County Council. The new trustees had little more success in attracting users. The original restrictions still applied and when, in 1926, a request was made for the hall to be used by touring companies 'catering for a good class of people', it was turned down, at the same time as clothing sales by a London firm were ended. Following temporary use as a sorting office during renovation of the Post Office in 1927, Miss Bailey opened a boys club, although the trustees were quick to ask for the 'removal of the lamp shades bearing a whisky advertisement'.

In 1938 the County Council were using the hall for cookery classes when, on the outbreak of war again, it became an ARP command post but not before the iron railings, which had adorned the property since 1846, were removed for salvage.

In the post-war years, pupils of Powells School became familiar with the buildings as an assembly hall and a place to enjoy the delights of school dinners, a bridge over the stream at the back providing access. This was almost the sole use of the hall until, in 1975 the physical conditions had deteriorated so much that the County Council terminated the tenancy and with holes in the roof and free-flying pigeons inside, the trustees sold the property to the Salvation Army, whose occupation a second time was not accompanied by rioting in the streets. Christopher Bowly's initials, high on the front wall, still overlook the Friends Meeting House opposite and, externally, the building is much as its founder constructed it, evidence of a very Victorian experiment in social improvement.

David Grace

Quaker meeting

The middle of the seventeenth century was a turbulent time in England, and political, religious and economic freedoms were key issues. Cirencester was a Parliamentarian stronghold in the Civil War and its capture by Royalists in 1643 was a major event in the history of the town. Institutional religion supported the status quo and served the interests of both power and wealth. (Punshon, 1984). In opposition to this, Cirencester's strong non-conformist background is evident from the several groups of protestant 'dissenters' who started to meet in the town at the time and to form congregations (Viner, 2002). The Baptists, Unitarians and Quakers all set up meeting houses for worship in the town within two years of each other in the early 1670s.

The Friends of Truth, now called the Religious Society of Friends (Quakers), was founded in Cumbria in 1652 by George Fox. From the 1640s like-minded people had come together from a variety of Puritan groups such as Baptists, Independents, Separatists and Seekers (Grace, 2002). Many came from the more political end of the spectrum of religious understanding. They did not consider that ultimate authority could reside in a church or an organisation. Nor did they regard the words of the Bible, or any other writing, as ultimate authority. Instead, they tried to enter into the spirit that inspired the writers. They believed in the equality of all people before God and so refused to remove their hats in the presence of their 'superiors'. A concern for truthfulness led Quakers, right from the early days, to refuse to take oaths, as an oath was an indication of two levels of truthfulness. In their Meetings for Worship there was no set ceremony and no set form of service. There were no priests, as all attending were equally able to contribute their thoughts, guidance and prayers. These principles continue today, as do the basic tenets of Truth, Simplicity, Equality and Peace.

The Quaker movement became known and spread across the country via itinerant preachers engaged in what they called 'publishing Truth', which was their way of describing their preaching of the gospel as Quakers understood it. These travelling Quakers or Friends included women and most came from the more comfortable sections of society (Punshon, 1984). They were not always welcome, were often met with hostility and many suffered beatings and imprisonment. These itinerant ministers set up a network of meetings across the country. Such meetings, with no building or clergy of their own to maintain, strongly objected to paying tithes to maintain the state church.

The institution of the Protectorate in 1653 should have brought relief to Friends from the persecution that 'dissidents' suffered, as they met the prescribed tests for tolerating religious sects. But this appears not to have been the case and many fell foul of the Blasphemy Act of 1650. Similarly, many travelling ministers were punished under the Vagrancy Acts dating from 1597, which allowed rogues, vagabonds and sturdy beggars to be flogged. In 1655 a proclamation required the taking of an oath in court, which meant that when Friends refused to do so, or to take their hats off in court, they could be charged with contempt and committed to prison for an indeterminate period (Punshon, 1984).

In 1651 a group of Baptists began to meet in Coxwell Street at the cottage of a widow, Joan Peltrace. The early members, half of them women, included a clothier, an ironmonger, a mercer, a shoemaker and a bodice maker. Baptism, by full immersion, probably took place in the river or possibly in the Gumstool Brook, behind the widow's cottage (Berkeley & Turner, 2000).

Quakerism in the Cirencester area began in 1655, with two women Quakers, who were travelling from the North, on their way to Banbury gaol to see Richard Farnsworth, one of the founding Friends, who was imprisoned there. They visited John Roberts of Siddington, a local Seeker, and held a Meeting for Worship in his farmhouse. John Roberts went with them to Banbury and spent time talking with and listening to Richard Farnsworth and, as a result, he was 'convinced' and became a Quaker.

A Quaker Meeting was established in the Cirencester area by 1656 and was held at the homes of Friends. George Fox, the founder, was a visitor to the Meeting. On the 12 August 1659 a burial ground was opened at Siddington, in the orchard of John Roberts' farmhouse, and his only daughter, Lydia, aged eight, was the first person to be buried there. The burial ground can still be found at Siddington, the site having recently been cleared.

The Quaker Act of 1662 and the first Conventicle Act of 1664 provided penalties for refusing to take an oath or encouraging others not to do so. It rendered illegal any religious meeting of more than five people other than a household. The penalty for the first and second conviction was a fine and for the third conviction, it was deportation. It was a grim time for 'dissenters'.

Their persecution eased toward the end of the 1660s and came to an end formally in 1672 when Charles II issued his Declaration of Indulgence, which suspended the penal laws against both 'dissenters' and Catholics and thousands were released from prison (Punshon, 1984). A year before this, the Baptists had built their first meeting house, on its present site in Coxwell Street and in 1672, the Unitarian chapel in Gosditch Street was granted a licence to worship. The building was converted into the new Cirencester Parish Centre in May of 2002.

On 1 May 1673, Richard Bowly the elder, cordwainer, and his son, Richard Bowly the younger, maltster, bought the lease on an area of land on the south side of Thomas Street in Cirencester, to build a Meeting House. The land, owned by the Crown, had been leased by Mary Rutter, widow, and by her daughters, Elizabeth and Margaret. The properties were transferred to the first Trustees, who included John Roberts' son. Friends in Cirencester subscribed towards the cost of building the Meeting House, and six preserved pages from a notebook of that date list their names with the amounts that they contributed. The original building was rectangular in shape (approximately 36 ft x 27 ft), with a door to the street which is still clearly visible – though it is now filled in. The Burial Ground behind the Meeting House was opened on 27 November 1673. Thomas Bamfield was the first person to be interred. The door to the Burial Ground remains and bears the date 1673 over the lintel. There are also remnants of a mullion window. This first building was modified in 1726, the date being recorded on the southeast corner. Perhaps a gallery was added at this stage; or, more probably, the large upstairs room, which ran the whole length of the original building, was added. This room was certainly in position before the alterations of 1810 and was used by the Women's and Children's Meetings. It now forms part of the Warden's accommodation.

Funds were raised again by voluntary contribution in 1774, when Cirencester Friends bought a tenement to the east of the Meeting House to build an extension, which doubled the capacity of the Meeting House. This was built in 1810-11 and cost £604 16s 4d. Three cottages to the east of the Meeting House were taken down to allow for this. The original mullioned windows, looking on to the burial ground, were enlarged by the addition of semi-circular heads to match those in the new extension. The present doorway added on the street side was constructed and the west wall of the original building was removed to accommodate the extension westwards. The exit from the extension to the burial ground bears the date 1810 over the lintel. The door from the street side through to the burial ground, presumably to allow access for coffins, is now closed off.

Some of the free standing benches date from the early days of the Meeting House and some are copies made at a later date; but the fixed benches, wooden panelling and the panelled passage between the old room and the new room, date from 1810.

A dwelling house adjoining the Meeting House was built at the time of the 1810 extension at a cost of £232 16s 9d. This is now the Warden's house. In 1828 Christopher Bowly, one of Cirencester Friends, at his own expense, had the cottage to the east of the Meeting House taken down, and erected an infant school room, with a cottage behind it, on the site. The date 1828 and the initials CB can be seen on the door lintel at the rear.

In 1865, £150 was spent on further additions to the front of the Meeting House. In 1874 there was storm damage to the Meeting House roof and this was reported in *The Gloucester Journal* on 4 July 1874. In the same year The Robert Brewin Trust was set up for the maintenance of the Cirencester burial ground.

Between 1870 and 1923 attendances declined to the extent that, by 1925, sale of the Meeting House was being considered. It was finally decided to keep it in repair and use it occasionally. Sarah Adlam Bowly, wife of a later Christopher Bowly who lived at Siddington House, undertook the care of the Meeting House until her death in 1931. John Gillett remained custodian of the burial ground. He died in 1947 and was for fifteen years between the wars the only Quaker living in Cirencester (Stephens, 1973). In 1936 the main room of the Meeting House was let to the Ministry of Labour as an Employment Exchange. The extension was used as a Reading Room for the unemployed.

In 1936 William Guest, a pacifist Methodist from Manchester, came to live in Malmesbury. He became a Quaker after working in France with the Friends Ambulance Unit. In 1937, he was joined in Malmesbury by a Friend, Stanley Hockey who came with his wife Marjorie, as geography master at the Grammar school. By 1938, there were Meetings for Worship once a month, when the manager of the Labour Exchange allowed them to use the office (the Meeting Room) with elders' benches and an old coke stove. The Meeting was rarely more than six at first. In 1939 Cirencester was once again a recognised Meeting of the Society of Friends (Stephens, 1973).

Friends Edgar Hope-Simpson, a general practitioner, and his wife, Eleanor, came to Cirencester in 1946 and the Meeting began to grow. The Ministry of Labour left in 1947. In 1947-48 the burial ground was turned into a garden with the help of five German prisoners of war and £50 from the Robert Brewin Trust. Edgar Hope-Simpson had got to know these young men in his capacity as official visitor to the prisoner-of-war camp at Siddington. They attended Meetings for Worship fairly often and formed friendships in the town, two of them marrying Cirencester girls (Stephens, 1973).

Displayed in the front entrance hall of Cirencester Meeting House is a Quaker Marriage Certificate dated 1863. The wording is the same as that used today. Sadly, the bride, Ellen Pumphrey, only lived for five years after the wedding and her gravestone can be seen in the garden.

In 1644 the *Directory of Public Worship in the Three Kingdoms* (which was intended to replace the *Book of Common Prayer*) abolished sacramental marriage and substituted a form of mutual declaration between the parties (Punshon, 1984). In 1653 Friends adopted their own procedures, which were not strictly legal until the Marriage Act of 1656 and were finally recognised at Nottingham Assizes in 1661. The form of the certificate, the making of the declarations and the witnessing by those present is still in use today. The Quaker marriage has survived unchanged for 350 years and is a procedure with a slightly different emphasis from those of other churches. However, Government is currently consulting on changes to the laws concerning marriage that may force a change. Quakers have been accused of spending too much time reviewing their history. Perhaps this potential change, so early in the twenty-first century, will serve to reinforce a basic Quaker concept that it is not the procedures that matter but the way we live our lives.

Much of this note is taken from a leaflet entitled *Cirencester Quakers, The Friends Meeting House, Thomas Street Cirencester*, written by Patricia E. Hawkins in 1995 and produced by Cirencester Preparative Meeting of the Religious Society of Friends.

References

Anon., *Quakers and Testimonies*. Quaker Home Service, London, 1990.

Berkeley, B., Turner, K. *A Narrow Cotswold Street. Coxwell Street 1250-2000*. Coxwell Street Residents' Association, Cirencester, 2000.

Grace, P. 'The Way We Were' in *Wilts and Gloucestershire Standard*, p.13, 8 August 2002.

Punshon, J., *Portrait in Grey. A short history of the Quakers*. Quaker Home Service, London, 1984.

Stephens, L., *Cirencester Quakers 1655-1973*. Cirencester Preparative Meeting of the Religious Society of Friends, 1973.

Viner, D., *Times Past* in *Wilts and Gloucestershire Standard*, p.14, 4 May 2000.

Jan Gronow

9 Pool and Porters

Cleaning the pool, 1977.

Pool of memories

Fly a glider over Cirencester and on the edge of Cirencester Park, tucked under the 'battlements' of the Old Barracks on Cecily Hill, you can see the turquoise rectangle that is one of the town's unsung treasures. Summer Sunday visitors to the Park will hear the give-away sounds of children's laughter coming from the rear of the Old Barracks, but to find this treasure, they have to retrace their steps back down Cecily Hill and follow the ornate old metal sign at the bottom of Thomas Street. 'Heated Open Air Pool, open May to September', it reads. A short walk beside a stream takes you to a footbridge, and the way in to the outdoor pool.

The unassuming entrance does no justice to the pool's lineage, for this is not only a local treasure for the fond memories it evokes. Cirencester Outdoor Heated Pool, opened in 1869, is the oldest pool in the country. Not only that, it has survived where so many others have closed. Its creation well predates the 1930s fashion for outdoor swimming and the lido boom – named after the famous outdoor bathing area in Venice. Our pool had been open sixty-six years by the time Cheltenham's Sandford Park Lido opened. Slowly the numbers have whittled down as local authorities have found them too expensive to run. In 1991 the number of outdoor pools and lidos in the country was 120. Now, just eleven years later, the number is down to fifty, with London's Brockwell Lido the latest to be under threat from cuts in local authority finance. So, not only is our pool the oldest, it is the oldest of a threatened species.

It too has been under threat of closure. In 1973 Val Jones was one of a nucleus of six people who banded together to prevent the council closing the pool. She lived in Gloucester Street, and her children attended Powell's school. Come rain or shine, she took them and a flask of cocoa to the pool after school where they all learnt to swim. It had been a delight to find the pool nearby when she had moved to Cirencester in 1969, then to her dismay, the closure was announced as the then new leisure centre was being built. The council claimed that no-one wanted to swim in the outdoor pool anymore and the District Engineers report referred to the need for expensive repairs. What the council hadn't reckoned with was the number of people who disagreed with them and their determination to fight. They raised enough money through jumble sales to pay for an independent survey which revealed that there was absolutely nothing wrong with the pool.

The team of six wrote letters to the papers. Val cycled around all the local schools collecting petition signatures – the driving concern for the Outdoor Swimming Pool Association as they called themselves was that children might never experience the joy of swimming outdoors if it was closed.

Thankfully, one councillor, David Grace, argued that 'these people must be allowed to present their case'. Their argument won the day and saved the pool from closure, but the council could not be persuaded to fund its upkeep. Instead they handed this over to the Association. But how were they to manage to keep it open? Anne Brocklebank came forward with a surety of £1,000 – 'a lot of money in the 1970s' – which enabled the group to take on the responsibility of the pool. So, in 1973 Bill Bowyer was featured in the local paper connecting the spring water source to fill the pool with water following an 'all hands in the pool' paint scraping and painting session.

Why did they bother, these six people? Florence Ellyatt, whose husband was the local barber, was in her sixties and shy of swimming in public. For her the early morning swim was a lifeline. She had no car and couldn't travel far. Swimming in the sunshine was a special experience, an amazing feeling. For Bill Bowyer it was because he was an avid swimmer. Becky Telling – married as Lucker – has a bench dedicated to her memory which records her fondness for a very special place. Of the other two, Russell Logan and Michael Lawlor, surely they were responding to the special qualities of swimming beneath the battlements and the line of Cedars of Lebanon under a blue sky.

Val especially remembers the blue skies of 1976. That blazing summer they made enough money on the turnstile to replace the men's cubicles that had stretched the length of the pool and so opened up the space there is today for sunbathing. She also remembers Florence Ellyot's personal contribution to fund raising. She had a very old fashioned pushchair into which she piled the unsold rolls collected from the town's bakers and pushed them around to the pool to make up and sell the next day. The irony is that in earlier times, Cirencester Urban District Council had itself

In aid of the Funds of the Cirencester Hospital,

(By kind permission of the U.D.C.,)

A

DISPLAY

OF

Fancy & Scientific

SWIMMING

AT THE BATHS,

ON

Thursday, 23rd inst.

At THREE o'clock, by

Stf. Sgt. C. S. SMITH

Poster for a swimming gala.

Summer at the pool, 1970s.

saved the pool from closure, having taken over the pool from the initial group of businessmen who had developed it as a private enterprise. They had approached Lord Bathurst for his help with their idea, which is how the meadow at the back of Barracks Yard came to be chosen. In 1884 a swimming club was formed, but the project began to founder due to lack of revenue for maintenance. The pool was filled with water from a spring and the coldness of the water was a disincentive to swimming. Try Stroud's lido for a taste of just how cold spring water can be!

The Council stepped in using the Baths and Wash-houses Act, once the District Surveyor had calculated that by 'raising the bottom of the baths by eighteen inches, it could be filled with warmer water from the mill stream by gravitation'.

Today's volunteers have family who worked at the pool then, so ties of affection are part of the attraction of the place. Barry, whom we have to thank for today's tuck shop, had a grandfather and uncle who worked as attendants. He remembers his uncle Fred telling him about emptying the pool every weekend. With no chlorination the algae grew rapidly in the summer. The pool was emptied on a Saturday night, then scrubbed clean on Sunday for refilling. Now that process takes a long time, as Barry knows from the days of annually scraping and painting the pool – a day to empty, a day to fill and another couple of days to clean with a power washer. So how was the process completed over a weekend? Boy power was the answer, many hands, many brushes, and the incentive – free swimming all the week long.

Barry is typical of the team of dedicated volunteers who maintain this unsung treasure on our behalf. He is passionate about the pool. 'It is such a lovely place. If you get there very early in the morning and sit around, the quiet is wonderful. It would be criminal to lose it.'

He swam there as a boy as much as he could after school and at weekends, though he did battle with his father on a Sunday, trying to squeeze his swim into a day packed with Morning Prayer, Sunday School and Evensong! Barry loved diving. There used to be a 10 ft board and across the corner a spring board, but, as he recalled, the best thrill was to run and jump off the roof of the entrance hut, 'we were diving into 4 ft 3in of water, but I don't remember any injuries.' And there was courting of course, 'I had several little flings with young ladies through the water polo gala held every Wednesday. We were in the West of England team. There was a lot of hero worship for some of those water polo stars. Not me, of course, I only made it into the 'B' team. I do remember that when we were kids, the wife of one of the council attendants at the pool ran off with the captain of the water polo team...'

Water polo and galas were a weekly feature at the pool. In 1912, the second of the annual 'Sports and Galas' was held and Miss Florence Tilton was the special attraction, promoted as 'the celebrated Lady Swimmer who will give two displays of her marvellous aquatic skill'. Was this display of Ornamental Swimming a precursor to the nose clips and fixed smiles of today's synchronised swimmers?

There were two open races then, with prizes of £1, 10s and 5s, presumably for first second and third place swum over 60 yards and 120 yards, Club Races and Comic Events. And the Gloucester City and Cirencester Water Polo teams fought it out.

The Gala was held on Thursday 22 August. Presumably this midweek timing was to avoid the twin evils of bitterly cold water at the start of the week and the filthy, stagnant, but warmer water of a Saturday afternoon?

Today there are no more galas as the pool's size, 30 x 15 yards, does not fit any modern event distances, but there is heated water. The 78° temperature is perfect for active swimming and the experience of swimming beneath the early morning sky, with no noise but the cries of birds and the gentle splash of water is a wonderful experience.

As well as being a testament to the dedication of generations of volunteers, the survival of Cirencester Open Air Pool into the twenty-first century is also a testament to the power of articulating our connection with special places. The pool is one of the town's very special assets. As Val says, 'Indoor pools are faceless and like thousands of others, but not the outdoor pool. Let's not let heritage slip through our fingers.'

So, as the 'new leisure centre or the 1970s' is about to be replaced by a new indoor facility, let's celebrate the longevity of our Cirencester Open Air Pool and look forward to a long future full of new memories to match Barry's thrill at seeing 'Tillo' Wakefield in full flight racing 'Rasher Scrivens' in a gala. Maybe we should celebrate our national treasure with a re-creation of that 1912 gala and begin a new era of fund raising to make sure that this one of the remaining fifty outdoor pools will be here to celebrate 200 years.

Jacqui Stearn

Off the rails
Prize-winning entry

For Ratty in *The Wind in the Willows*, life without the sights and sounds of the river would have been unthinkable. In my childhood and formative years, to have lived without the sights and sounds of the railway is unimaginable. Born in 1943, I lived with my

Aerial view of Watermoor station, 1950s.

parents and elder brother, Michael, in No. 2 Nursery Road, a small cul-de-sac in Watermoor, off Siddington Road, abutting the railway embankment of the former Midland and South-Western Junction Railway. At this time it was a busy line with two tracks taking vital supplies from Cheltenham to Southampton. It also provided the German Luftwaffe with a useful route to return home after raids on the north and Midlands.

Watermoor developed as a community at the southern end of the town during the Victorian and Edwardian eras. It was here that the first gasworks was built in 1933, taking its coal from barges on the branch of the Thames and Severn canal coming into town from the junction at Siddington. In 1883 the Watermoor railway line was opened and in 1895 the M & SWJR works was built on land to the west of the Watermoor station. The railway provided work for many in Cirencester and also led to the building of housing such as the red brick terrace of the original Midland Road. The buildings of the

works lingered on to the 1970s, mostly roofless, but the works itself moved to Swindon in 1925. With the iron foundry on the Swindon side of Watermoor bridge, Watermoor was a somewhat industrialised part of town, a tradition perpetuated today in the development of Love Lane.

I am told that in 1943 I was often put outside in my pram, ably protected by Ruffy, the Rickards' family dog from next door. Doubtless the sounds of the steam engines, pulling their carriages and trucks of wartime passengers and supplies registered in my subconscious.

The sound of steam however could have been the last sound I ever heard when, at the age of three, I followed the lead of my worthy brother with his fourteen months more experience of life. He decided to take me 'to see the wheels go round'. I remember nothing of the considerable climb up the embankment, just of standing by the sleepers of the down line as a large engine sped towards us hissing and steaming. Fortunately a neighbour in his garden at the rear of the

Watermoor station looking towards Swindon, 1964.

houses in Siddington Road saw us, jumped the wall, dashed up the embankment and grabbing one of us under each arm, scrambled to safety as the train passed. We never again ventured on to the line, although occasionally we balanced on the wire boundary fence to scrounge sweets from the patients in the ambulance trains which called in at the station. These must have been casualties being brought back from abroad as the war had been over for at least a year. The profits from these activities helped to augment our sweet ration which we collected each week from Barber's shop in Watermoor Road. Often my mother would tow us up to the shop from Nursery Road on the large wooden steam engine made by father. My one and only memory of

the town station at this time was when my mother took us up to see the Royal Train at the station when the King and Queen visited in May 1946. Watermoor was very much our domain.

We remained registered for our rations at Barber's even after we moved house to No. 81 Chesterton Lane, in October 1947. We needed extra space to accommodate the imminent arrival of younger brother David. This move did not take us away from the railway as our new home was only about 100 yards west of the Chesterton Lane railway bridge, where the lane crossed the Kemble to Cirencester Town branch line. The houses in this part of Chesterton Lane are semi-detached and were built in Cotswold stone by the

Railway cottages in Midland Road.

council at the end of the First World War. Ours was in the second block from the bridge with the luxury of a gas street light outside the front door. The bridge itself was faced with Cotswold stone with a narrow roadway crossing it. The footpath was so worn down by traffic as to be almost on a level with the road surface.

We had very long gardens which ran parallel with the railway lane and beyond the gardens was an area of wasteland which had once been a paddock, but during the war had been cultivated as allotments in the 'Dig for Victory' campaign. Many of the gardeners had long since given up digging for victory so the children in the area adopted it as our playground, christening it 'The Long Grass'. It was bounded on its eastern side by a sleeper and wire fence, then a ditch known colloquially as 'The Fever Ditch'. This was supposed to be a drainage ditch for the railway bank, but some unofficial connections had been made to it which gave it a very

unsavoury appearance and smell at certain times of the year. Beyond the ditch was the bank still protected by barbed wire entanglements left by the Home Guard and beyond this the cutting with the single track. Nearly all our, non-school, waking hours were spent here, except for most Saturday mornings.

Despite having moved away from the Watermoor Line I had a friend at the Council school in Lewis Lane whose father worked on Watermoor station and it became a regular Saturday morning feature to go down to the station to 'help' the porters. This was of course unpaid work and before the days of Health and Safety and the litigation culture. The station had two tracks and two platforms and to get to the shelter on the Eastern platform passengers had to cross by a wooden sleeper crossing north of the main platform. There was a similar arrangement to the south, to be used only by authorised staff. We considered ourselves authorised and often crossed it carrying goods off the train to the main platform, even sometimes having great fun rolling such things as tractor tyres across the line.

Even more rewarding was a visit to unload a train in the goods shed, which was a corrugated iron building on a siding by the remains of the old works and Howard's coal yard. The early 1950s still being the age of steam meant that when the engine moved in or out of the shed, the smoke and steam from it brought down large quantities of rust and soot from inside the shed roof. While this created very evocative sounds and smells it also covered the clothes of the 'junior porters'. Our parents always knew when we had been to the station on a Saturday morning. We also came back with quantities of leaflets from the waiting rooms offering day trips and excursions to exotic destinations on the English Riviera.

At this time there were only two private car

owners in Chesterton Lane between the bridge and Somerford Road but we had the luxury of the railways and used them as naturally as you would a car today. The most convenient route to Swindon for shopping was via Kemble, so we used the Town line mostly. On Wednesdays during the school holidays the huge railway works at Swindon were open-house to children. Here we collected engine numbers and stood and watched as whole engines crossed over our heads on conveyers, no hard hats or thoughts of health and safety again. I often wonder what the workers thought of these regular invasions.

One day near the end of a summer term around 1954, the Watermoor station had its own invasion. It was customary for the older children from Lewis Lane school to visit London by train going via Kemble and Swindon main station. However, on this occasion we boarded a train at Watermoor and went all the way to Southampton via Swindon

The rail bus leaving Cirencester town station.

Chesterton Lane Halt.

Old Town, Savernake and Andover. We then boarded the ferry boat Medina to Cowes on the Isle of Wight. On the return journey we sailed back on the *Balmoral* which evidently still takes passengers on cruises in the Bristol Channel. In my class alone there were fifty-four children, heaven knows how the teachers and helpers coped, but I know we had a great day out which sadly could never now be repeated.

Eventually enthusiasm for life as a junior porter waned, probably to the great relief of all the Watermoor station staff, but I retained some interest in the line as I had transferred from Lewis Lane to the Grammar school in 1955 and the line ran on the embankment by the side of our playing fields. One member of the staff, Mr Geoffrey Romans, normally a strict disciplinarian, but also a keen railway enthusiast, would often stop our English lesson to see which engine was pulling the train that day, *Cookham Manor, Granville Manor*

or one of the Southern Region engines with shields on the side of the boiler.

In the latter days of the line when Chedworth station was unmanned we took a class trip by train to the Roman villa. For the return journey our teacher, Miss Doris King, had to hail the train like stopping a passing bus or taxi. The driver, seeing her waving wildly, deliberately drove beyond his proper stopping place with a smile on his face. Away from school, our interest lay more with the Town Line now as Terry King, the elder brother of Derek, one of our 'Long Grass' gang, was now working at the station, training to be a driver and eventually turning the dream of many a school boy or retired vicar into reality. We knew everyone who worked the line either by sight as they passed by, or by name. It was a typical branch line and we had needed little imagination when our teacher had read us the story of the Railway Children at the junior school.

Football was another obligatory activity of growing youth and the Long Grass provided ample scope for this and a safe place to play, until the ball went on to the railway line. In hindsight railway safety comes to mind, but at least in those days you could hear a steam tank engine coming and there were no deadly electricity cables. In the event every precaution was taken and we did know the railway time-table as well, if not better than, the May family's dog next door, who ran down the garden path every time a train went by. To retrieve the ball however three of us would cross the ditch and fence on to the railway bank, one remained to watch for approaching smoke and listen for any unexpected train. The other two would negotiate the Home Guard barbed wire, then one would put his or her head on the track to listen for the vibration of a train while the other looked for the ball (do not try this at home!)

In those days it was unthinkable that a town like Cirencester could flourish without a railway and hindsight proves it. In the mid 1950s work commenced on refurbishing the Town station, the gaslights installed in the 1800s were replaced by electric lights and work commenced on altering the parcels department. Such perverse behaviour by a government department should have raised suspicion. However in 1958 came a new innovation, forty-six-seater diesel rail cars took over from the steam passenger trains. Halts were constructed along the line including Chesterton Lane Halt, below Chesterton Lane bridge. A footbridge was built alongside the parapet to ease the congestion on the bridge and all seemed set fair for the future. We could travel into town for 3d, or, if we put the oil lamps on the posts on the halt and at the top of the path by the entrance gate, Vic Rose, the guard, let us travel free.

In the 1962/63 winter, my last at school, so much snow fell over the Christmas and New Year that with the freezing conditions which followed, the snow stayed until March and for three weeks in January the town was completely cut off by road. The only vehicle able to get in from the outside world was the diesel bus. Every morning, as paper boys for Bailey & Woods, we collected the papers from the train and pulled them through the snow in town to the various shops, using a porter's trolley. My training had paid off.

Sad to say, in 1964 Mr Marples, the Minister of Transport, aided and abetted by the strange financial and statistical analysis of Dr Beeching, announced the imminent closure of both of Cirencester's railways. Despite some vigorous opposition, notably by Vera Pope, the date of the last passenger diesel bus was set for Sunday 5 April 1964. Driven by George Williams, from the Welsh Valleys, it set off for Kemble at 11.30 p.m. with a wreath bearing the tribute 'Killed by Marples' attached to the front. I along with my brothers and a full passenger compliment travelled on the train for a last nostalgic journey. On the way back protesters had fixed fog detonators to the line and back in Cirencester Vera Pope burned an effigy of Ernest Marples on the pavement outside the station. My brothers and I played in the Salvation Army band in Cirencester, as did George Williams, so when the railway closed we lost our trombone player and of course the end of the railways meant the end of so called secure jobs for a number of other employees.

The Town station, a listed building, now stands forlorn and virtually unused except for the ex-railway WC. Watermoor station is completely obliterated save for concrete Home Guard tank traps by Kingsmead which once went from the Eastern platform to Bridge Road bridge. A few of the trees which lined the station entrance still stand in a factory car park next to the foundry. Along the line of the Grammar School embankment and on the bank of the remains of the cutting, between Meadow Road and Somerford Road, are still some of the Home Guard picket stakes in position. The railway can never be as it was, but maybe someone of vision might be persuaded to build one from Somerford Road and Love Lane junction to Kemble where the Cirencester platform still waits for a ghostly train. For myself I can sit in my garden in Sperringate, on what was the canal bank and listen to the roar of traffic on Guru Buchanan's relief road one garden away, but late on a summer or frosty winter's night, when the traffic has ceased, I can sometimes hear a train at Kemble or is it a ghostly reminder of yet another instance where this town has progressed backwards?

Peter Grace

In memoriam

The 1960s were something of a watershed in the architectural development of Cirencester's centre with the opening up of the central area now known as the Forum, with the new police station, Forum car park and its entrance roads. South Way, West Way and North Way replaced an area of gardens and random buildings which had been inaccessible to the general public. Many of the buildings on the south-west side of Dyer Street between Gloucester House and the Market Place came under the demolition contractors' hammers to be replaced by the Dyer Street development. Anyone with historical sensitivity or appreciation of Cotswold architecture must cringe at this pile of reconstructed stone perched on plain concrete pillars. The obsession with this relatively new, cheaper alternative to Cotswold stone pervaded many of the building schemes at the time.

Sadly, in this feverish desire to 'modernise', a number of historic and architecturally interesting buildings were sacrificed. The Abbey House, which had been considered as possible new municipal offices, was demolished in favour of the more commercially exploitable private flats. Let's face it, it hardly makes sense in these days of 'open government' to have municipal offices in a central position easily accessible to the public. At around the same time the original

The original memorial inscription.

The Cottage Hospital, 1913.

Mullings Court disappeared from Dollar Street, along with Dyer Court and its Doric colonnade in Dyer Street. Another substantial building to go was on the north-east side of Dyer Street, the Congregational church and its extensive useful schoolroom and ancillary rooms. Opposite the London Road end of Dyer Street was the Gaumont picture house and theatre, a wonderful period piece with balcony and boxes. When left derelict, the stage displayed a backdrop of a huge picture of Cirencester Market Place which must have been used on many a special civic occasion. This backdrop eventually fell victim to the elements because no-one thought fit to save it or offer it to someone who would have cared for it. It seems that even today this attitude can creep in when commercial consideration takes precedence over public amenity. The Regal cinema is probably soon to go the same way and the former Town Station, although a listed building, seems destined to fall into dilapidation through lack of use and minimum maintenance. It will probably not be long before it is labelled an eyesore and interested parties push for its

removal to open up commercially profitable land.

Of more significance to the town however is the proposed destruction of the remaining parts of a building which has served the population for well over 100 years. In Sheep Street stands the Old Memorial Hospital, built in 1875 and presented to the town by the then Major Allen Bathurst, later Earl Bathurst. Its first designation as a memorial came at this time as it was built as a memorial to Earl Bathurst's first wife Meriel Leicester Bathurst, the daughter of Lord de Tabley. An inscription to this effect can still be seen above the main entrance although at the time it was called the Cottage Hospital. The building was described in those early days as 'a picturesque half-timbered edifice in the mixed style of art prevalent between the decay of Gothic art and the Classic revival.'

Architecture aside, the hospital was run by a committee of fourteen local elected men and women with the running costs raised locally from annual subscriptions, donations at fundraising events including the annual carnival, collections from churches and fees

Carnival in Dyer Street.

levied on individuals according to their means and at the discretion of the board. These were the days before the National Health Service, but this hospital with its seven beds served the community which supported it well. In the first ten years around 950 cases were dealt with, many requiring great surgical skill and careful nursing. There was a resident matron and nurse and the town's doctors gave their services free. In 1913 local philanthropist Daniel Bingham financed a new wing which increased the number of beds to twenty and it became known as the Cirencester Hospital. Within a year the First World War had started and Cirencester was allocated the task of providing medical care for wounded servicemen. Most of these were cared for at the Bingham Hall which was turned into a military hospital for the duration. It was here that the relatively new skills of X-ray photography were introduced into the town. Today the Memorial Hospital building still retains a tangible connection with this war as

the magnificent wooden staircase which now leads to the upper floor and the room where civil marriages are solemnised was presented to the hospital in memory of a casualty of that war. Major Edgar James Bannatyne, DSO, commander of the 38th Training Squadron of the Royal Flying Corps stationed at Redcombe in 1917, died in the hospital from his injuries after leaping from his burning aircraft over the airfield. It is said that his courage and charming personality had made him one of the hospital's most popular patients. His parents in Limerick, Ireland, were so impressed by the efforts made by the medical staff that they presented the staircase to the hospital in his memory.

After the war the hospital took over the Apsley Hall on the opposite side of Sheep Street. This had once been an independent chapel, one of whose pastors in the 1800s was the father of Jerome K. Jerome, the writer of *Three Men In a Boat*. The X-ray and electrical department were installed in this building along with nurses' accommodation on the first floor. The frontage was carved with the names of those of the town who died in the First World War and this new addition gave rise to a new name, Cirencester Memorial Hospital, one which it retained until its demise as a hospital in 1988. Patients being wheeled across the pedestrian crossing from the main building to X-ray must often have been a little disconcerted by the inscription, on the façade above the upper windows on the front of the building, which reads 'To The Memory of Our Glorious Dead'. By 1925 the hospital could boast a 'perfectly-appointed operating theatre, an electric lift from the lower to the upper floor, and a bacteriological laboratory'. There were now twenty-six beds for adults and children and a wooden building which could be used as a sanatorium or for isolation purposes, although the latter was catered for on the larger scale by the Isolation Hospital, known colloquially as 'The Fever Hospital', in Bridge Road. This had been built in 1878 to replace a 'Pest House' originally situated in

land used in the building and layout of Holy Trinity Church, Watermoor Road. In 1931 another major extension to the main hospital took place to increase the capacity to forty-three beds at a cost of £10,000. An unusual addition made during the Second World War was the air raid shelter which was built in the garden in 1940.

The war led to a considerable increase in the temporary and permanent civil population within the town which made increased demands on the hospital facilities. In 1940 a twenty-four-bed evacuee children's hospital was established over Smith's seed merchants shop in Cricklade Street. Daisy Bracher was the sister in charge and it was administered from the Memorial Hospital as was an adult evacuee clinic at the Hostel at No. 2 Querns Hill. Sad to say the increase in the number of road accidents necessitated the building of a new emergency mortuary in Querns Road. This red brick structure was to augment the hospital's own mortuary just inside the North Gate. The latter is shown on the photograph

The sand bagged Hospital, 1940s.

The wartime staff, 1945.

of a parade passing the hospital during the war. It also shows the sandbag wall which was built up to first floor level so that seriously ill patients could be kept in the building during air raids. The others would be moved to the shelter in the garden, the north entrance of which was set at an odd angle to accommodate a chute which projected patients down to the shelter from the first floor women's ward. There were three-tier bunks along the inside of the west wall of the shelter and with these and the benches provided, the shelter could accommodate eighty people. Every time the siren sounded an air raid warning the shelter was manned and occupied. This occurred over 200 times and on one occasion the warning sounded at 4.54 a.m. but the all-clear did not sound until 3.05 a.m. the next day. This must have been a very trying time. Hospital staff, however, were ably assisted by members of the Cirencester Red Cross detachment who gave

invaluable help. Emergency lighting for the hospital in those days was provided by a generator in Bridges Garage in Castle Street and the ambulances were garaged in the Cotswold Garage buildings off the entrance to what is now Cripps Road. While most of the military casualties in the area were dealt with in military hospitals, on at least one occasion over thirty injured paratroopers were brought in for treatment after their glider crashed on a training exercise from RAF Down Ampney while training for the D-Day landings in Normandy.

During the war the maternity facilities for Cirencester were actually in Tetbury and at one time the Biddulph family offered Rodmarton Manor as an alternative for post-war Cirencester. However, this was thought to be still a little far out from the town. On the other hand the 'Querns' private house, Tetbury Road, had been requisitioned during the war for use as a nursing and convalescent home for babies who were casualties of the Blitz. With the help of public subscription and local initiative, the Maternity Hospital opened in 1948, four days before the inception of the National Health Service. It had twenty-one beds and was administered from the Memorial Hospital. It is rather annoying to think that when it closed in the late 1970s it was the National Health Authorities who did the deed without much reference to the townsfolk who had set it up in the first place.

At the time of the creation of the maternity hospital and for many years before, geriatric care had mainly been provided at Watermoor Hospital which had been known as the Public Assistance Institution and before that the Workhouse, which opened in 1836. However, in 1975 Watermoor Hospital closed and the geriatric patients were moved to a new building at the Querns. By this time the Isolation Hospital in Bridge Road had become an annexe of the Memorial Hospital mainly for convalescence.

In 1988 the rest of the Memorial Hospital uprooted and moved to the Querns site leaving just the building on the west side of Sheep Street to become the Memorial Centre, dealing with occupational therapy and mental health matters. The main hospital building remained intact until bought by the Cotswold District Council in 1989. To facilitate more in-town parking much of the back of the building housing, amongst other things, the pathology department, women's ward, private wards, nurses' day room, boiler room and mortuary, were all demolished and a car park set out. The air raid shelter, thanks to the intervention of a number of influential individuals such as the late General Sir John Hackett of Arnhem fame and bodies such as the Imperial War Museum, was saved from demolition. The CDC then gave permission for the Living Memory Historical Association, a local charitable trust and the group who initiated the saving of the shelter, to take it over for use as a public exhibition venue. Each summer since 1989 they have presented an exhibition of wartime memorabilia with the aim of illustrating

The former Cottage Hospital, 2002.

life in the Cotswolds during the war, making special reference to the work of the local civil and military hospitals. The trust also recently planned to take over the former casualty department in the main building as a research and study centre, a plan that has been put on hold while the hospital's fate hangs in the balance.

Much of the building has had no permanent occupation since the closure of the hospital but the front ground floor area and part of the first floor have been used by the registrar for marriages and, by now, hundreds of couples have taken advantage of this facility so that it means a great deal to many in the community outside its valuable hospital service. The main frontage still maintains it original character and is an ideal setting for weddings. Cirencester College has also been using rooms for computer training, a bus company uses part of the 1930's extension and the CDC themselves have used the former male ward on the first floor for conference and training purposes. It is to be hoped that unless the town wishes to see another example of short-sighted action, this time for a small increase in parking facilities and income, people of influence will do all they can to prevent the former hospital's demolition. The town cannot afford to lose any more buildings of such character and in this case one which could so easily be used for community purposes, to some extent honouring the gift made to the town by Earl Bathurst in the first place.

Peter Grace

10 Around Cirencester

Replicas of the 'Cerney Head and Foot'.

Hidden treasure

Many of England's parish churches as well as cathedrals, are the custodians of treasures of great variety. Some are of gold, silver, silver gilt, pewter, and some are jewel encrusted. They include Communion plates, chalices, lavabos and alms dishes. Some are of so much monetary value that they are kept in bank vaults because the churches no longer dare keep them in their often inadequate safes and have problems with the insurance premiums. Sadly, churches are no longer respected by thieves. But there are other treasures which

have a value beyond money and which form integral parts of our churches, such as exquisite wood or stone carvings and ancient wall paintings. One such treasure is in the church of All Hallows in the village of South Cerney, on the southern edge of the Cotswolds, in Gloucestershire.

In 1913 some internal alterations were being carried out near the tower. This involved the part demolition of the north wall. It soon became clear that behind the wall facing was a cavity. Further exploration revealed that the cavity held a small, carved head and foot and a pile of wood dust. Both

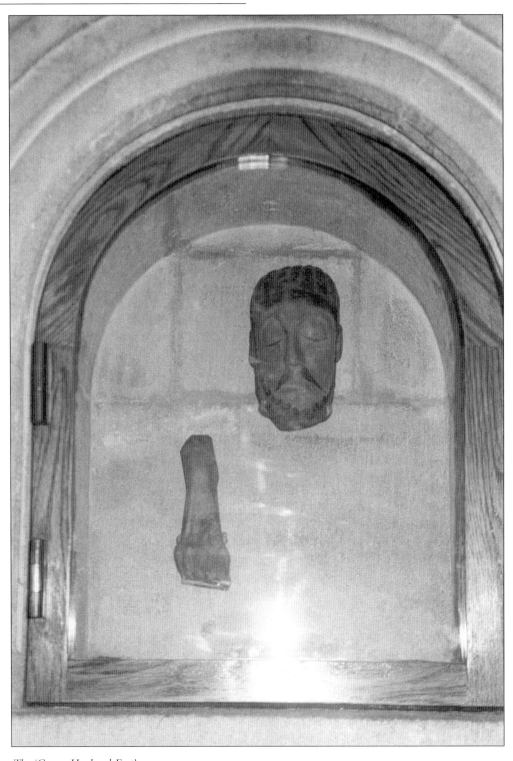

The 'Cerney Head and Foot'.

the head and the foot were about five inches long, and in a parlous state. In particular, the head was wafer thin and clearly would soon have gone the way of whatever it was that had turned to dust on the cavity floor.

It did not take much deduction to realise that the two artefacts had once been part of a crucifix, and it was but a short step on the part of those who discovered it, to connect that crucifix with a bricked-up rood loft above the eastern end of the main aisle. The only means of access at that time, and indeed today, to the rood loft was by ladder. But a simple calculation showed that the crucifix would have been about half life size, the same size as the bricked-up space; in fact, a perfect fit.

The people present when the discovery was made were Fred Harding, a South Cerney stonemason, his assistant Bert Cox, also a village resident, and the vicar's churchwarden Mr E.T. Cripps. Mr Cripps decided to make enquiries in the British Museum and to this end took the head and foot to London in his pocket after having first partly filled the head with sawdust and glue in an effort to make it stronger.

It was soon established that the artefacts were the remains of a twelfth-century rood of English or more probably Spanish origin, a question which has not yet been settled. They were also agreed to be amongst the oldest and most important pieces of carved wood in the whole of Europe – a find indeed in an English parish church.

The discovery seems to have made less impact on the village than it would have done today, when experts from all over the world would have descended on the church, accompanied by radio and television. All that really happened was that a glazed niche was cut into the wall below the tower near where the head and foot were found, the spot being marked by an incised cross. In the niche the two little objects were mounted on metal brackets. When, some years later, the electricity supply was connected to the church, there was a switch to illuminate the niche for the benefit of visitors. A small booklet was written outlining what was known of the history of what became known as The Cerney Head and Foot, and offered for sale for a few pence. So time passed and all the while the Head and Foot were deteriorating. Then, in 1983, the Parochial Church Council received a request from the British Museum which was mounting an exhibition of artefacts of historical interest from the past 1,000 years. Could the museum borrow the head and foot to use it as part of the exhibition? The answer was 'yes' and so they were taken to London where it soon became clear that they were in a dire condition. So much so that, in the interests of history, they would have to be kept under strictly controlled conditions of temperature and humidity, or they would be lost forever.

To this end the British Museum proposed that the remains be housed at the museum on permanent loan, renewable every five years. The PCC agreed, realising that it could not provide in the church the appropriate conditions or the necessary insurance cover in view of the monetary value which was placed upon the precious objects. Also the museum offered to provide in their place a polyester resin copy, to the layman's eye indistinguishable from the originals, plus an artist's impression of what the original crucifix would have looked like, as well as history of the relics as far as it was known. So today, the church can display its 'head and foot' and a history of these rare and precious relics. The copies are proof against damp and cold, while the originals are safely housed in London for the appreciation and edification of many more scholars and of future generations than could ever be expected in South Cerney. At the same time they are, and always will be known as The Cerney Head and Foot.

Now the British Museum has purchased the

An artist's impression of the original crucifix.

Cerney Head and Foot. As always in such cases there had to be a Consistory Court hearing which parishioners were entitled to attend before the permission could be given. There was much soul argument, but eventually it was agreed that the village was in favour and the decision of the Diocesan Chancellor was that the sale could go ahead. The price agreed was £60,000. This amount was paid to the Diocese of Gloucester, but the interest is available to the Parochial Church Council to help with the maintenance of the church fabric.

The story though does not end here, there are too many loose ends and questions which will always be asked. When was that crucifix first brought to the church in this small village? There are no records of a gift or sale. Who was responsible for bringing it and possibly giving it and what reasons did he or she have? The church at that time was, as were all our churches part of the Roman Catholic Church. That is assuming that it was in the church before the Reformation which is surely a safe assumption. Where did the crucifix come from? Ask three experts and you will get four answers. Perhaps the most intriguing question of all is how did it come to be inside the hollow wall? Somebody must have put it there and presumably with a really good reason for doing so. Given the conditions of even a couple of hundred of years ago it was a decision which would have been made only after a great deal of serious thought and indeed, trepidation. Such religious articles were not treated lightly. It is probably safe to assume that it was hidden for its own safety and two periods in our history when religious artefacts were in danger of being destroyed, were the Reformation and the Civil War. The latter has left its mark on many churches in the Cotswolds in the forms of empty niches which once held statues as well as the marks of cannon and musket balls. So did someone hide the crucifix in that hollow wall to protect it from such danger? If so, whoever it was must have been prevented from returning to disinter it, or even to pass on the secret to someone else. Whatever the answers to these questions we must be grateful that the relics were discovered and that they have now been saved from further deterioration and made available for future generations to admire and be intrigued by them.

The legend supplied by the British Museum describing the two fragments rhapsodises about them. It refers to the time when they were displayed at the Hayward Gallery in the Arts Council of Great Britain's Exhibition of Romanesque Art 1066-1200: 'the head stood out as one of the masterpieces of English Romanesque – one of the supreme periods of English Art'.

Pay a visit to All Hallows church and see for yourself. You will be moved by the expression of loving resignation on the face and the agony of the pierced foot. The questions may still remain but so do the Cerney Head and Foot and they are still much loved by the people of South Cerney.

E.W. Fletcher

'The Cotswolds – I love it, I want it in America!'

It was love at first sight for American car magnate Henry Ford when he was introduced to the Cotswolds. The visit was arranged by his wife, Clara, a native of Warwick, during a brief trip to Europe. Ford was enthusiastic about the architecture of the region, which he felt characterised an idealised way of life, with picturesque cottages nestling amid colourful gardens. The whole scene, he said, provided a wonderfully restful image. The more he saw the more he enjoyed… and he gradually began to develop an astonishing dream. What

Rose cottage (1620) in America.

if he could transport a complete Cotswold village, stone by stone, timber by timber, across the Atlantic and set up such a scene in the heart of his own homeland?

As one of the richest men in the world at the time, Ford considered such a task was not beyond him. He had a ready reply for those who ever doubted his more eccentric notions: 'Money talks… if you want something bad enough you just have to offer the right amount'.

For some time Ford had been playing with the idea of setting up his own version of London's Science Museum, which he greatly admired, on his land on the outskirts of Detroit, Michigan. He intended such ambitious plans to serve as a tribute to his great friend, Thomas Edison.

Ford was born in 1863 on a family farm. His family had moved to America from Ireland but could trace their roots to Somerset. He began his working life in Detroit machine shops, moved on to become an engineer with the Edison Illuminating Company and then concentrated his considerable energy to the manufacture of motorcars. His famous Model T Ford began life in 1908 and the rest, as they say, is history. Part of Ford's museum plans included the erection of historic structures, such as original homes and workshops of famous Americans. He also planned to set up vintage machines, crafts, furniture and, as he was to explain, 'anything that catches my eye'. That eye, as it turned out, would wander over the Cotswolds.

In 1928 Ford came to England to check out the progress of a search he had initiated for examples of James Watt steam engines. 'I would like some for my museum' he admitted. A report had been drawn up for him by Herbert Morton, an engineer at the Ford plant in Manchester, who had been touring the country trying to find old Watt engines. The couple met at a London hotel and within a few minutes Ford calmly announced he was prepared to spend 'around ten million dollars buying up bits and pieces for my museum' and so began an astonishing six years for the retiring Manchester engineer. What had started as a brief meeting in a London hotel room for a chat about steam engines developed into a bond between the two men. For the next half dozen years Morton took on the role of Ford's chauffeur, secretary, buyer and companion. Ford instructed his accountants to 'give Morton anything he wants', with the result that day after day he set out with up to £1,000 in cash crammed into his pockets. Not once did he see Ford pay for anything personally. 'I don't think he ever carried any money with him', Morton was to say later.

When the two men were not tramping together around the streets of London, stopping to buy clocks, musical instruments and whatever else took the American's fancy, they were driving around the country, often miles off the beaten track. The Cotswolds came in for an intense exploration, particularly villages around Cirencester and further afield, taking in Fairford, Bourton-on-the-Water, Lechlade and Moreton-in-Marsh.

At one time Ford and his wife had considered buying a property in the heart of the Cotswolds to serve as their base when they came to Europe. When pressure of business killed off this idea, Ford then considered the possibility of buying 'a complete Cotswold village' and having it shipped over in its entirety to his museum site in America. He became fascinated by stories he had heard about Bibury, a village close to Cirencester. What, he wondered, had stirred William Morris to write, back in the 1870s, that this was the most beautiful village in England? He confessed that he began to understand when he saw Arlington Row, overlooking a water meadow on the River Coln, for the first time. He looked in admiration at the steeply pitched stone roofs of the cottages and was enthralled to learn these one-up, one down, former weavers' homes had been converted from a former monastic barn. 'What a remarkable sight these cottages would be in the States!' he said. 'We will take the complete row over there!' The properties, he felt, would make an idea focal point for a 'typically English village scene' in the museum. 'I will buy a Cotswold church from somewhere else around here to complete the picture', he added. But Ford failed with both ambitions. When his ambitious scheme leaked out in the Cirencester area there was an immediate public outcry. 'If the locals are upset by this plan' said Ford, 'perhaps they will let me take down just one end of Arlington Row and take that'. But no, they most certainly would not. Ford's plans caught the attention of the Royal Society of Arts and the cottages were saved by Gloucestershire Archaeological Trust and in 1949 given to the National Trust.

Public protests were also made when it was revealed Ford had his eye on Winchcombe parish church and wanted to take it down and ship it across to America. The imposing church tower would, he said, 'make a lovely sight near Detroit'!

Despite Ford's belief that 'money talks', he had to admit defeat over Arlington Row and Winchcombe parish church. 'Just keep looking', he told Morton. And that is just what the Englishman did. He admitted he lost count of the miles he travelled, the villages he visited, in his quest. And then, one day, he happened to be driving through another village close to Cirencester when his attention was drawn to a sixteenth-century cottage. Morton recalled later that 'lights flickered through leaded windows… it looked just like the scene from a Christmas card. I knew I had found the cottage I was looking for.' Morton was hesitant about knocking on the door of a complete stranger and announcing that an American millionaire wanted to buy the cottage. He decided to drive on and think about the problem later. How strangely fate can work at times. The next day Morton was walking past the window of an estate agent and saw a notice about the cottage being for sale. Rose Cottage was being offered for £500.

Morton was so convinced he had found the right property for Ford that he bought the cottage on-the-spot for the asking price. He sent his American boss photographs and details about the building and waited with fingers crossed….

The reply was prompt: 'Love it – send it over'.

It was then that Morton discovered major problems. A builder found a number of rotting timbers and said in his expert view the cottage could never be taken down and rebuilt. So Morton gave instructions for all the rotting wood to be replaced – and then for the cottage to be dismantled! That is exactly what happened. It took local craftsmen seven weeks to take the building apart. Every piece of stone, every scrap of wood was numbered and carefully stacked away in packing cases and specially constructed sacks and moved by road to Stow-on-the-Wold railway station. The 175-ton load was then taken to London docks in a special train consisting of sixty-seven wagons. After being shipped across to New York, eighteen freight cars moved it all the way to the Detroit museum site.

Ford then sent a cable to Morton: 'If Cotswold craftsmen took the cottage down, I want Cotswold craftsmen to put it together again. Send them over.' They made the trip and it took them two and a half months to sort out the piles of numbered items and put the cottage back together again. To ensure he had managed to capture a 'complete Cotswold picture' Ford also had plants and shrubs from the original Chedworth garden transported to Detroit along with some Cotswold sheep and doves for the dovecote. Mr and Mrs Ford were so pleased with the final result that they sent the Cotswold workmen on an expenses paid trip to Niagara Falls before they returned to England.

Ford later also bought a derelict Cotswold blacksmith's forge from the village of Snowshill and had that shipped out too, complete with nails from the floor and rusting tools. Mr and Mrs Ford frequently entertained guests at their 'Cotswold Home' with Mrs Ford baking cakes in the old oven. They did, however, also express sadness that they had never managed to transport Arlington Row!

Bill Charlton